Dear Samantha +

Q you might enjoy this study.
a friend of mine wrote this
book + I did the study. It's
great.

Metamorphosis of the Mind:
Experiencing Jesus as the Truth

I love you.

Love, Mom

Day One

The way my mother tells it, somebody climbed up on the stove to reach the cabinet with the cookies in it. She could tell because the fish food had been spilled all over the stovetop. So she lined the three of us up to determine the truth.

"Gayle, was it you?"
"No, ma'am."
"Glenn, was it you?"
"No, ma'am."
"Jeanne, was it you?"
"No, ma'am."

"Well, come here. I want to show you why you shouldn't do this…. it's dangerous. You see, if you were to climb up here and accidentally step on these buttons, it would turn the stove on. And then if you stepped over here onto the eye, you'd burn your foot!"

Being only four and not very bright, I quickly responded, "But I didn't climb up over there, I climbed up on *this* side!"

Busted.

I've never been very good at lying. *I guess, I'm just not smart enough to carry it all the way out.* Somehow I end up talking myself into a corner and the truth comes out.

Oh what a tangled web we weave, when first we practice to deceive. —Sir Walter Scott, from his poem, Marmion, 1808.

I'm not a good liar. There is one thing, however, at which I sometimes excel. And that is this: believing lies. I can be gullible and naïve at times, especially if the lies are attractive— if they are something I *want* to believe.

I've heard it said that Satan has no new tricks— that he always uses the same old weapon: Deception. Scripture calls him the "Father of Lies." He *used deception in the garden against Eve, and he will use deception until his time on earth is finished.*

Look up Revelation 20. You can see in verses 3, 7, and 10 the practice Satan uses in his attempt to destroy God's people.

Satan's purpose is to deceive. He attempts to deceive nations as well as individuals.

Satan never tries anything different. His weapon has always been, and will always be deception.

Beth Moore writes:
Satan will be loosed for a short season at the end of the millennium and be allowed one last stand. His deceptions will resonate with the minds of proud men who will want to believe him, and they will foolishly gather with him against the King of Kings.
1
I certainly don't want to be one of those *"proud men"* who *"want to believe him."* I want to recognize deception quickly and reject it.

In John 8:32 Jesus says, *"Then you will know the truth, and the truth will set you free."*
Truth sets us free.
Lies keep us in bondage.

I want to be free.
How 'bout you?

We are surrounded by lies, my friends. Lies are everywhere!

- On billboards - *"Use our product and then you'll be happy."* (Just like the models who were paid thousands of dollars to let us take this picture. Of course they're happy!)

- On television - *"Parents are really idiotic and should be ridiculed. Kids are the smart ones and should certainly never be disciplined for their smart aleck remarks."*
- From Hollywood – *"Love happens when two really good looking people see each other for the first time."*
- In magazines – *"Ten pounds in ten days…lose it quick before the holidays!"*

What are some prevalent lies you recognize as part of our culture?

_____

_____

_____

Hosea 4:6 says, "My people are destroyed from lack of knowledge."

Look up that same scripture in *The Message* Bible. *(You have a scripture index for each day's verses.)*
Complete the following from *The Message*:
My people are ruined because they don't know what's _____ or

_____.

We must know truth, or else be ruined, destroyed, by our own sin.

Funny thing about lies…sometimes it's not easy to know they are lies. They are deceptive (imagine that!). They are sneaky and tricky and slippery. So one of the most important things we must learn is simply this: *How to recognize a lie for what it is…**not true***.

Our goal for this study will be to do just that: to look at individual lies people tend to accept as truth, and—using the Word of God (our only source of complete truth)—expose them as deception.

Remembering that Jesus said, "You will know the truth and the truth will set you **free**," Our ultimate goal will be to know the truth, and allow that truth to set us free from bondage.

Freedom in Christ.

Freedom from the deception of Satan.

That's our goal.

Metamorphosis of the Mind:
Experiencing Jesus as the Truth

Day Two

I went to a retreat one October. There were decorations all around; you know how ladies retreats are. There were pumpkins and colorful leaves and candles, fall-time stuff like that. However, leaning against the speaker's pulpit there was this big stuffed, pastel-colored Easter bunny.

Toward the end of the retreat the speaker asked if we saw anything odd about the decorations. Of course, the Easter bunny issue came up. Her explanation was ~~very~~ telling. "We should be able to recognize when Satan is lying to us just as quickly as we recognize that the Easter bunny doesn't fit here."

She went on to say, "If someone were to walk through that door over there and begin to speak to us in Chinese, we wouldn't understand him. That's what Satan's lies should sound like to us—like a language we don't understand." We ought to shake our heads and say "Nope! I just don't understand that kind of talk! That doesn't compute in my brain. That doesn't line up with my thinking. That is not part of my belief system."

Isn't that the truth! When Satan tries to lie to me, I would love to recognize immediately that it is his voice yammering in my ears. I would love to be completely deaf to the enemy's lies.

One way to combat Satan's deception is to be so preoccupied with hearing what God is whispering that there's no room for Satan's voice. Isaiah says, "Your ears will hear a word behind you, 'this is the way, walk ye in it,' whenever you turn to the right or to the left." This has always been one of my favorite scriptures. I love the idea that the Lord is continually directing me by murmuring instructions to me as I walk throughout my days.

In order for my printer to actually print a document from my computer, the printer cable must be plugged into the computer's USB port or the wifi has to be connected. I can't tell you how many times I've tried to print out a document only to sit and wait while nothing happens. I always get frustrated, thinking something is wrong, until I realize "Oh yeah,

it's not hooked up." The connection has to be made between the laptop and the printer before the printer will do its thing. Imagine that!

I want to be so connected to God, that Satan finds no port to plug into, right? I want to be closely communing with my Father, so that Satan cannot find a way to connect with me. Wouldn't it be great if we were so full of the truth of God's Word and His love that there would be absolutely NO ROOM for the lies of the enemy?

Jesus spoke to his disciples—not in the language of computers—but in a language they could understand. He spoke of a Vine and branches. He encouraged his disciples in John Chapter 15 to "Remain in Me, and I will remain in you." He said, "Apart from Me, you can do nothing."

IVP New Testament Commentary says, "The main point of the image is clear enough: the intimate union of believers with Jesus. The disciple's very life depends on this union."

The disciple's very life depends on this union. We must be intimately united with Christ, remaining in Him, abiding in Him, in order to hear His voice and bear fruit. So what does that mean: to remain…. to abide?

In the original language this is the word ***meno***, which means "to remain, abide, dwell, endure, last, to persevere, continue, tarry…"

There is a sign on my living room wall that reads: "Sit long, talk much." That is tarrying— sitting long and talking much. I love to have friends hang out in my living room and visit with me. That is the way we need to be with Jesus—spending MUCH time in His presence, listening to His voice, communing with Him, letting Him speak His love to us, allowing Him to sing over us.

Practically speaking, how does one do this? What methods do you use to connect with God?

_____

_____

_____

How can you maintain that connection throughout a busy day?

_____

_____

_____

I will forever emphasize the importance of having time scheduled and set apart daily to spend with God. It can be called many things: quiet time, devotions, appointment with God. I don't care what you call it, just *do it!*

Do it, my friends…somewhere in your busy schedule, you must find time to quiet your thoughts and meditate on Jesus. ***It will revolutionize your life.*** Spending time with God will change the way you see things. It will help you know truth and recognize lies.

Even Jesus Himself spent time alone with the Father. Look up the following scriptures:

- o Matthew 14:13
- o Matthew 14:23
- o Mark 1:35
- o Luke 5:16

Choose one of the four verses and copy it here:

_____

_____

_____

_____

If Jesus Himself needed to find a time and place away from the busyness of His life to spend time alone with the Father, how much more do we need to do this?

Day Three

Y ou can lie to yourself that the lie isn't really a lie.

What?

I said, you can tell yourself, "Oh this isn't really a lie, this is true." Even though you know good and well it's a lie.

This, my friends, is called denial…. and it's not a river in Egypt. Satan loves to draw us into denial. It's more deception!

The way to learn to recognize counterfeit money is to examine the real thing for so long, with so much diligence, that you see the flaws in the counterfeit bill. That's what professionals do in order to learn to identify fake currency. They know every detail of the genuine article so that any discrepancy is evident.

If you and I want to be able to identify Satanic language as the deception that it is, we have to be well versed in speaking truth. We've got to know the truth of the Word of God if we're going to recognize when Satan is trying to twist and manipulate it. The more we read and study scripture, the more we will be able to see through Satan's tricks.

I worked at a school where students were required to grade their own school work. They took their papers to a scoring station where they compared their answers with a score key. This system was based on complete honesty. The students had to be honest about whether their answers were right or not, and they had to mark their papers with a red X if they answered incorrectly, and then go back to their desks and correct their work.

It was very tempting for students to change their answers at the scoring station instead of taking the time to mark the work wrong and then correct the answers back at their desks. Sometimes students who had been dishonest at scoring would convince themselves they were taking a 'shortcut'. A shortcut is generally thought to be a good thing. These students convinced themselves that lying was a good thing because it helped them finish quicker. However, their dishonesty at the scoring station almost always became known when they took tests and didn't know the correct answers.

In the same way, you and I are living in denial if we don't pay close attention to the thoughts we believe. If we believe Satan's lies, we will fail when the tests of life come.

In John 17:17, Jesus prayed,
"Sanctify them by the_____, your word is _____."

Charles Spurgeon wrote:
*The truth is the sanctifier, and **if we do not hear or read the truth, we will not grow** in sanctification. We only progress in sound living as we progress in sound understanding. "Thy word is a lamp unto my feet, and a light unto my path." (Psalm 119:105)…Hold fast the truth, for by so holding the truth, you will be sanctified by the Spirit of God.[2] (Morning and Evening, p. 384)*
(my emphasis).

The only source of complete truth is the Bible. The Word of God alone gives us absolute and comprehensive truth. So then, it stands to reason that if we want to live according to truth we must read, study, and believe the Bible. This goes hand in hand with yesterday's lesson about spending time regularly with the Lord.

"The sovereign Lord has given me an instructed tongue, to know the word that sustains the weary. He wakens me morning by morning, wakens my ear to listen like one being taught." Isaiah 50:4

Are you a wife? A mother? A friend? Sister? Co-worker? Do you ever come into contact with weary people? Weary husbands? Weary children? Weary friends? Weary co-workers? Here's a way to encourage those weary people around you: Get up when you hear God calling! Let Him waken you morning by morning. Then find a quiet place to spend time alone with Him.

Complete the following scripture:
And you will seek Me and _____ Me, when you search for Me with Your
_____ _____. Jeremiah 29:13.

It's a promise! When we *seek* Him with our whole hearts, we will *find* Him! That's amazing! That's awesome! That's so worth getting up for! Or staying up late for! It doesn't matter what time of day you do this. Just do it. You know better than anybody when you are able to truly focus on the Lord. Morning, evening, nap time—there is no right or wrong time. There is no right or wrong way. Just do it. Spend time with God. Ask Him to reveal Himself to you. He promises He will do it.

What time of day works best for you to have an appointment with God?

- o Morning
- o Afternoon
- o Evening
- o Night

My challenge to you is this: If having a regular daily quiet time is not already a part of your schedule, determine right now to make it one! This decision will change your life and, therefore, the lives of those around you. God's Word promises this to be true.

Day Four

I can be very easily distracted. I can start out doing one thing and, before I get it done, find myself doing something altogether different. You know, I head through the house toward the kitchen, to take something out of the freezer to thaw for dinner. On the way, I see shoes that need to be put away so I take them to my closet. There I see all of the laundry that needs to be done, and so I end up in the laundry room starting the washing machine…and dinner never gets thawed. Good thing we have microwaves.

One morning as I was emptying the dishwasher I realized that I had a method, a routine, about how I put dishes away. I do it in a certain order. First the silverware, then the bottom rack, then the top rack starting with the small cups and glasses and ending with the mugs. I have a specific method for doing this. And it occurred to me, a routine keeps me on track. It helps me not get distracted. I may get sidetracked, but having a routine helps me stay focused.

I have this daily morning routine that I think is super important. The first thing I do after I get out of bed and brew some coffee, is find a warm and comfortable place in my home where I spend time alone with God. It's as much a part of my routine as getting dressed or brushing my teeth. This is something I feel very strongly about. I believe that if we are to have a vibrant, exciting, living relationship with the Lord, we have to spend time with Him! And the best way to make sure you do that is to make it a priority, part of your daily routine—just like getting dressed in the morning.

As I mentioned yesterday, **when** you have a quiet time is not the issue. I like early mornings. Some people like late nights. Find whenever it is that your life quiets down a bit. If you are a mama of young children, it may be during their nap time. If you work full-time, it may be during your lunch break. It doesn't matter **when** you do it…but it does make an incredible difference **if** you do it.

Moses spent habitual time with the Lord. It was part of his regular daily routine. He did it consistently and on purpose.

Read Exodus 33:7-11. NLT

Fill in the blank.
It was Moses' _____ to take the Tent of Meeting and set it up some distance from the camp.

It was Moses' what?
His _____.

Let's do a little vocabulary work here:

Practice – "to do something as an established custom or habit."

So, Moses had this established habit—something he did regularly and on purpose. He went to the _____ v. 8.

According to verse 9, what would happen with the pillar of cloud when Moses went into the Tent of Meeting?

_____

_____

What did the people do while this was happening?

_____

_____

11 Inside the Tent of Meeting, _____ _____ _____ to Moses face to face, as one speaks to a_____.

Wow! Do you want the Lord to speak to you? I do!

Do you want to be called a friend of God? I do!

This was part of Moses' routine:
o   He went.
o   God came.
o   They spoke as friends.

And this affected the people of Israel! The example of their leader made them hunger for God!

10 When the people saw the cloud standing at the entrance of the tent, they would stand and bow down in front of their own tents.

I believe that when we, as parents, make it a habit to have a quiet time, it affects our children. It has to impact them when they come down the stairs every day to find their mama or their daddy spending time with the Lord.

When parents seek God, children benefit. When husbands seek God, wives benefit. When wives seek God, husbands benefit. When employees seek God, bosses benefit. When bosses seek God, employees benefit. Seeking God's face not only helps us, it benefits others. The people around you will be blessed.

Metamorphosis of the Mind:
Experiencing Jesus as the Truth

Day Five

We make appointments with our doctors, barbers, friends, bosses, and sometimes, because life is so incredibly busy, we have to make appointments with our spouses. . . just to make sure we'll have time for them!

List people with whom you make appointments:

_____

_____

_____

_____

Have you ever thought of making an appointment with God? Have you thought of setting up a standing appointment with Him, knowing that when that time comes, you're going to stop everything else and just be with Him? Here's the thing about doing this with God, He will never stand you up. He'll never forget. He'll never even be late. *He's waiting for you* to draw near to Him!

Fill in the blanks using James 4:8 from the NASB.(you have a scripture index) _____

_____to _____and He will _____ _____to you.

Scripture says that when we choose to draw near to Him, He will draw near to us. Scripture also says that His nearness is our good. . . so it must be a good idea to set up appointments with God.

The word for "near" in the Greek is **engizo** and it means "communion with God in prayer and the desired and cherished fellowship with Him".[2] (New Testament Lexical Aids)

Look at those adjectives... *desired... cherished*—describing what?

Fellowship with God!

We make an appointment with God, not because we *have* to, but because we *want* to…it's our desire to be with Him. It is out of love that we do this, because we like being near Him. Spending time in His presence is so beneficial to us.
The Psalmist writes of this in Psalm 73:28 NASB.

But as for me, the _____ of God is my _____;
I have made the Lord GOD my refuge,
That I may tell of all Your works.

What is a refuge? That's not a word we use much in today's language. How would you describe it?

_____
_____
_____

I think of words like sanctuary, safe place of rest, no conflict, a shelter. In the midst of the everyday struggle and strife of life in our world, isn't it nice to know there is a place of safety where we can go and rest? Not a physical place, but a place we can go in our spirit and find peace.

You will keep in perfect peace
all who trust in you,
all whose thoughts are fixed on you!
Isaiah 26:3 NLT

Peace comes when we fix our thoughts on God. We can find peace and safety in His presence. Doesn't that sound like a good place to be?

Is anything keeping you from seeing God's presence as good and safe?

_____
_____

There are lots of different names for this: quiet time, devotions, daily Bible readings, vespers. You can call it whatever you want to call it, just please make sure that you are doing it. Life can be so difficult, and having a friendship with God can make the frustrations of this world easier. This is one of the most significant habits you will ever develop.

I wonder if this scripture might mean as much to you as it does to me.

Now as they observed the confidence of Peter and John, and understood that they were uneducated and untrained men, they were marveling, and began to recognize them as having been with Jesus.

Acts 4:13

Isn't that amazing? Peter and John actually looked different because they had been with Jesus! They gained confidence because they had been with Jesus! People could look at them and tell that they had spent time in His presence!

Do you ever have trouble with a lack of confidence? A low self-esteem?

o Never
o Sometimes
o Always

Spend time with Jesus! This scripture indicates you'll gain confidence from being with Him.

Is there something in your life that you are concerned about today? Something that is robbing you of peace? Are you lacking confidence because of a particular issue today? Take a few moments and express that concern to God. He is waiting to hear from you, waiting for you to draw near to Him. He promises to meet you there.

Conclude today by writing out your prayer to Him. After you've expressed your concern, leave it in His oh-so-very-capable hands.

_____

_____

_____

_____

_____

_____

_____

_____

Day Five

_____

_____

_____

_____

_____

Metamorphosis of the Mind:
Experiencing Jesus as the Truth

Day Six

My granddaddy lived in Coosa County, Alabama for several years after his retirement. He had been a pharmacist in the college town of Auburn, Alabama, and, after retirement, moved to the country community of Speed, Alabama. He and Nanny bought a house just down the highway from my Uncle Billy.

Down the road from Nanny and Granddaddy's house lived an old black man named Mark. Granddaddy and Mark became best friends. They did everything together. Every day they worked together cutting wood, fixing fences, and feeding the hogs. They did whatever needed to be done, and they did it together. They were such good friends.

In January of 1981, Granddaddy died unexpectedly. An aneurysm burst and he passed away. I attended college in Manhattan, Kansas at the time, and I remember our family loading up in the car and heading down to Alabama to go to the funeral. The long drive was filled with stories of spending time at Nanny and Granddaddy's house.

What happened the night before the funeral is forever in my memory. We were at the funeral home for the visitation, and I saw Mark standing over the casket where my granddaddy lay. He was so very sad, and as he stood there looking down, he said over and over again, "He was a good man. He was a good man." It broke my heart to see Mark grieving.

The year was 1981, but this was rural Alabama. Although the civil rights movement had taken place two decades earlier, it still was not accepted in this southern country culture for a black man to go into a white man's church. Mark knew that he would not be able to attend the funeral the following day. This visitation was his only opportunity to say goodbye to his best friend.

The next day Nanny, Mama, and Uncle Billy got into the funeral home limousine, and the rest of us climbed into cars to follow them to the service. As we drove past

Mark's house on the way to the church, I looked over. . . and there, standing in his front yard. . . stood Mark. He was dressed in his Sunday suit. He had his hat in his hands, and he bowed his head as we drove by. To honor his friend. Mark knew that he could not come to the funeral that day, that it would not be acceptable. But he took the time to get up and get dressed anyway. Out of love for my Granddaddy.

And I think what Mark was saying through his silent actions that day was this: "I don't care about man-made traditions and rules, Mr. Phillips, you are my friend. Your friendship is very valuable to me. You are worth the time and effort it takes for me to get dressed up and come out here to show you this respect. You are worth it. Our friendship is worth it."

When we have a daily quiet time is it pleases our Father. He wants so much to spend time with us, speaking His grace and kindness over our lives. As we set aside time to be with Him I believe He is blessed. He enjoys the company of His beloved children. He wants to be our friend.

The first relationship God had with man was a **friendship**. Scripture tells us that Adam and Eve walked with God in the cool of the day in the Garden of Eden. They hung out together. They walked with each other in the cool of the evening—until that lying snake came and ruined everything. Yet, even still, God made a way for us to be friends again. Glory to God, I'm so thankful for that!

I think when we make the choice to get out of bed early, or to stay up late, to spend some alone time with God, what we are saying is this: "Lord Jesus, my friendship with you is valuable, you are worth any effort. I *want* to spend this time with you. Our friendship is worth it." Much like Mark did for Granddaddy, we can say to our Father, "You are worth it."

You may be saying, "How in the world can I be a friend to God? He is the almighty, omnipotent, powerful God of the universe...and I am just an ordinary woman."

I would love to show you scriptural evidence that being your friend is exactly what that almighty, omnipotent, powerful God of the universe wants.

"Come now, let us reason together," says the LORD. "Though your sins are like scarlet, they shall be as white as snow; though they are red as crimson, they shall be like wool. --Isaiah 1:18

Come to me, all you who are weary and burdened, and I will give you rest. Take my yoke upon you and learn from me, for I am gentle and humble in heart, and you will find rest for your souls."

--Matthew 11:28

What do you say to a friend? I say, "Come! Come over to my house! Come meet me for coffee! Come on, let's go, I want to be with you!"

That's exactly what the almighty God of the universe is saying to you in these two verses: "Come, let us reason together…come to Me…"

When I sign birthday cards to my closest friends I like to use descriptive words to tell them how I feel about our friendship. What descriptive sentiments does God use about you in Isaiah 43:4?

_____

_____

_____

_____

What is a common thread in the following verses?

James 2:23
2 Chronicles 20:7
Isaiah 41:8

_____

_____

_____

Abraham is called _____.
Don't you think God wants to call you that, as well?

In Luke 7:34, Jesus is called a _____ of tax collectors and

_____.

I'm certainly a sinner. I guess that makes Him my friend, right?

We spend time with our friends because we want to. In the same way, quiet times will become a routine in our lives when we do them—not out of compulsion, not 'should' or 'ought to,' but instead, "I can't wait to be together again…. to get into Your Word and see what You have to say to me today. I want to be with You today."

He is your friend, not because you have a quiet time. You want to have a quiet time, *because* he is your friend.

The reason that Granddaddy and Mark were such good friends was because they spent so much time together. They did a variety of different things during the course of a day. When I encourage you to have a daily quiet time, I'm not saying you need to do a two hour Bible Study every day, I'm just saying that when you set aside a time that is special—a time you know you'll be sharing with God—you're creating a foundation for the rest of your day. With Jesus on your mind, you will face your day with confidence and joy. And the side benefit is: you're building a friendship with God!

Metamorphosis of the Mind:
Experiencing Jesus as the Truth

Day Seven

God's presence is a place of blessing and protection. There is a story in the Old Testament that perfectly illustrates this. To the Hebrew people the ark of the covenant represented the very presence of God. This ark was a box in which special remembrances were kept, things that reminded the people of the Lord. Inside were the Ten Commandments, Aaron's rod that budded, and a jar of manna. This ark was so important to them that they took it with them even when they went into battle.

The NIV Compact Bible Commentary reports:

*The ark was a wooden chest overlaid with gold. It was handcrafted by Israelite artisans during the period of desert wanderings. The pattern for building the ark was given to Moses at Mount Sinai, and it became one of the most important components of Israel's worship. By means of the ark, the invisible presence of the God of the covenant was visualized. **The ark was no mere symbol of God's presence. It was the place where God had chosen to center his presence among his people***.

At one point in history, the ark was captured by the Philistines. While the enemy had it in their possession, they tried to place it in their idol temple. God has a great sense of humor. Their idols literally fell on their faces in the presence of the ark of the covenant. You can read 1 Samuel 5:1-5 if you're interested in this account.

Some time later the Philistines left the ark for the Israelites to find. King David and a large group of men went out to rescue it and bring it back to Jerusalem. David and his companions were very excited, rejoicing with exuberance that the ark was being returned. However, they failed to follow the rules God had given about moving the ark. They transported the ark on an ox-cart. The oxen tripped and a guy named Uzzah reached out to keep the ark from falling, and God instantly struck Uzzah and he died. Right there on the threshing floor. See this for yourself in 2 Samuel 6: 2-15. This really scared David. He decided to give up on their plan to bring the ark back. He was freaked out by this and said, "How can I ever bring the ark of God to me?"

Scripture goes on to say,

He did not take the ark to be with him in the City of David. Instead he took it aside to the house of Obed-Edom, the Gittite. The ark of God remained with the family of Obed-Edom in his house for three months and the Lord blessed his household and everything he had.

The Lord blessed Obed-Edom! And his household! And everything he had—just because they were storing the ark of God. This is amazing to me. Obed -Edom didn't ask for this responsibility, he simply happened to live nearby and have a place where the ark could be stored. And the result? Blessing!

God's presence brings blessing, my friends. It's the truth. Being in His presence blesses us and our households.

If you follow this story a little further, you'll find that this event changed the course of this man's life.

Some time later, after David had done some construction in Jerusalem, he prepared a place for the ark and pitched a tent for it. Following the guidelines God had established, David called together the Israelites and they went, once again, to bring the ark of God to the City of David. This time they were successful in bringing the ark back.

Read 1 Chronicles 15:23-24. Do you see a familiar name listed?

_____

What was his job to be?

_____

Read 1 Chronicles 16:4 -6. Obed-Edom is mentioned again. What is his job description in this passage?

_____

The direction of Obed-Edom's life was changed because of the presence of God! Not only was he blessed along with his whole household, but he experienced a mid-life modification because the ark of God was randomly placed in his home for a season! Nothing is ever random with God, dontcha know.

Spending time in God's presence can be a little bit risky. You may find the very course of your life altered because of relationship with Him. It's pretty exciting, if you ask me. I want to be challenged! I want to be changed! I want whatever it is that God has for me. And somehow, I suspect that you feel the same way.

The presence of the Lord also provides protection. Look up Psalm 91:1 and copy it here:

_____

_____

_____

The Hebrew word for 'dwell' used here is **yasab**, meaning, "to sit, dwell." Used literally or figuratively, it can indicate a lengthy residence, a short period of waiting or a temporary visit.

Any amount time at all that we choose to spend in God's presence is going to be of great benefit to us. This passage goes on to describe the protection provided to those who dwell in God's secret place.

Read all of Psalm 91. List 5 ways God promises to protect us:

_____

_____

_____

Psalm 91:15 is written from the Lord's perspective. Copy it here:

_____

_____

_____

A daily quiet time provides a forum in which we can call upon Him. He promises to bless us and protect us. As we stay with Him, listening to His voice, we will become so familiar with truth that we'll be able to quickly distinguish lies, and therefore reject them. Please join me in this amazing, life-altering habit of daily "sitting" with the Lord. It will change our lives.

Five Benefits to a Daily Quiet Time

Day Eight

We were in one of those all-you-can-eat buffet style restaurants. Six year old Maggie had finished her required number of "real" foods, so I allowed her to go back for dessert. After multiple tastes of cookies, ice cream, cake and pie, with her tummy crammed as full as could be, Maggie climbed into her daddy's lap. Face to face with her dad she proclaimed, "I've never met a morsel of icing I didn't like!"

Beth Moore says when we get our emotional needs met by time spent with Jesus, then any affirmation another person may give to us is just whipped cream. It's extra! **When Jesus is my satisfaction, I don't require others to meet my needs.** My husband, my children, my friends don't have to be my need-meeters because my needs are met!

When I get up in the morning and spend time with God, I am giving Him an opportunity to pour His love out on me, to lavish His amazing love all over my spirit, so when my family gets up...my emotional needs have been met! My emotional tank is full. John doesn't have to pour affirmation into me, because I've already been affirmed. So anything he may add is simply whipped cream! It's the icing on top! I don't walk around needy, looking for people to build me up with encouragement, because my God—the lover of my soul—has already filled my emotional tank. I am satisfied by seeing His likeness each morning.

Look up Psalm 17:15 in the scripture index and fill in the blanks:

15 And I—in righteousness I will _____ _____ _____; when I awake, I will be _____ with seeing your likeness.

Isaiah 58:11:

11 The LORD will guide you always;

he will _____ _____ _____ in a sun-scorched land

and will strengthen your frame.

You will be like a well-watered garden,

like a spring whose waters never fail.

The Lord is the One, my friends…the only One who can truly satisfy our needs, amen?

Song of Solomon 2:14b:
Show me _____ _____,
  let ____ _____ your voice;
  for your voice is sweet,
  And _____ _____ is lovely.

This last scripture is spoken from God's perspective toward us. He wants to see our face and hear our voice. The number one benefit of a daily appointment with God is that having a quiet time provides **satisfaction**.

Secondly, a regular quiet time with God provides **a connection to the power source**. As mentioned in Day Two, my printer must be synced to my computer in order to print. By the same token, the computer must be plugged in to a source of power in order to even turn on! The plug has to be in the outlet. Otherwise, nothing happens when I push that button.

"I am the vine; you are the branches. If a man remains in me and I in him, he will bear much fruit; apart from me you can do nothing." John 15:5

Jesus is the vine; we are the branches. We MUST be connected to Him to have life! We are totally dependent on God! We MUST have Him! In the phrase, "apart from Me you **can** do nothing" the word **can** in Greek means *"to be able; have ability."* Without Jesus we have no ability, and we can accomplish nothing for the kingdom of God.

Jon Courson writes:

We need to be in His presence daily, in His Word continually. If not, we'll cut off the flow of sap that would have produced fruit for His pleasure and rewards in eternity…an irrefutable fact of spiritual life is that every man, every woman is only as close to the Lord as he or she chooses to be. And if you choose to abide in him, to intertwine your life with His, to wrap yourself around Him and stay close to Him, you will inevitably bring forth much fruit.

Having a time set aside each day to spend with Him is like getting charged up—connecting to the Power Source. Even as I have to plug in my cell phone to let it charge overnight, I need to spend time connected to *the* Power Source in order to be effective for Him. I must stay connected to the source. Jesus is my source.

This third benefit is actually the one that is most related to the goal of our study. A regular quiet time helps us to **renew our minds.** The scripture this entire study is based on is Romans 12:2:

Do not conform any longer to the pattern of this world, but be transformed by the renewing of your mind. Then you will be able to test and approve what God's will is—his good, pleasing and perfect will.

Be transformed by the _____ of your _____.

It's a Metamorphosis of the Mind. Look at this scripture in the NLT:

Don't copy the behavior and customs of this world, but let God transform you into a new person by changing the way you think. Then you will learn to know God's will for you, which is good and pleasing and perfect.

Changing the way you think! That's our goal, friends—to change the way we think! Instead of thinking and believing lies, I want us to be transformed, metamorphosed to the point that we no longer believe the lies of the enemy, but we choose instead to believe truth.

There is only one way to do this. There is only one source of complete truth: the Word of God. You're doing it. Right now, you're being transformed, because right now, as you open His Word, you are studying the one source of undeniable truth. I'm so proud of you.

Ephesians 5:26 reads: "...Christ loved the church and gave himself up for her to make her holy, cleansing her by the washing with water through the word."

Through the washing of the water of the Word, we renew our minds. The Word of God is truth, our greatest and most sure source of truth. When we believe God's Word, we are believing truth. When we meet with God and study scripture, we are telling ourselves truth. We are tearing down the lies that have become so entrenched in our brains that they seem like truth to us.

Concluding today's lesson, let's review. **A regular quiet time with God provides:**

1. Satisfaction

2. A connection to the Power Source;

3. A way to renew our minds.

Tomorrow we'll touch on two more benefits. I look forward to meeting you here!

Metamorphosis of the Mind:
Experiencing Jesus as the Truth

Day Nine

Wondering what you're supposed to do? Where you're supposed to go? How the Lord wants you to invest your time? A daily quiet time gives us a forum in which to seek God's will.

Yesterday we concluded that a regular quiet time with God provides:

1. Satisfaction

2. A connection to the Power Source

3. A way to renew our minds

Let's look at a few more benefits today. First, a regular time with God provides **direction**.

Your morning quiet time is like a military briefing. It's where you will receive your orders for the day.

Look up Psalm 119:105 and fill in the blanks:

Thy word is a _____ to my_____ and a_____ for my _____.

It's translated in the Message this way:

"By your words I can see where I am going; they throw a beam of light on my dark path. I've committed myself and I'll never turn back from living by your righteous order."

I realize that much of our lives are planned for us. We have these responsibilities and routines that we carry out every day. We have to do laundry; we need to go to the grocery store. There are basic requirements that are part of our way of life.

Some of us go to work, others stay home and teach children; there are unlimited variations in our lives.

Much of your life is already scheduled for you. However, in the midst of whatever that routine is, I believe with all my heart that God arranges "divine appointments" for you daily.

I believe that all along the way, in the midst of your day, God wants to use you to affect other people. That's why it's so important to commit that day to the Lord! A quiet time provides an opportunity for us to ask God to guide every errand, every encounter, and to use us for His glory.

Sometimes what I'd really like from God is a five-year plan. I want Him to give me a detailed layout of what is going to happen and when. Notice how this scripture says His Word is like a lamp. Think with me for a minute about a Coleman lantern you might use when you're camping. When you walk through the darkness with a lantern, the light only illuminates a few steps in front of you. I think many times, that's the way it is with God's will. He lets us know what He wants just a few steps at a time. Yet all along the way He is guiding us. When we check in with Him daily and commit our way to Him, we can be sure of His guidance.

Although there are countless benefits to meeting with God, we'll make this the last one. A quiet time is an *expression of our submission.* This is where we say, "Today, Lord, I *choose* to follow You. Today I will say, 'yes' to Your plan. I bow my knee to Your sovereignty today. You are God and I am not."

This is huge! This admission of our dependence on His loving care lays the foundation for our day. It puts us in a place of recognizing our need for a Savior, a Director, a Protector. He is all of these things and more. When we have a quiet time we are, in essence, saying, "Lord, You are all of these things to me…You are my Savior, You are my Director, You are my Protector. In everything that happens today I am thankful You are present. I need You so much."

Spending time with God and acknowledging Him as your Savior, Director and Protector will change the way you see life. You will begin to see things from a different perspective. You will begin to worry less and trust more. You will begin to fear less and relax more. As you spend time with God, you will become convinced that He is in control and watching over you, and that there is, indeed, nothing to worry about!

The Bible is filled with examples of God rescuing people out of messes of their own making. As we spend time reading the Bible and we see these examples, we realize that He is able to do the same thing for us. We read about Shadrach, Meshach and Abednego and we realize that God will walk with us in the fiery trials of our life. We read about the disciples in the middle of a storm at sea, and we realize that Jesus will be with us through the storms of our lives. Reading about how Jesus reached out to tax collectors and prostitutes reassures us that nothing bad we do will separate us from His love. So we fear less and trust more. Spending time in His Word is vital.

Real quick, let's review. A regular quiet time with God provides:

1. _____
2 _____
3. _____
4. _____
5. _____

Now, if you don't currently have a regular quiet time I'm not trying to turn this into some kind of legalistic requirement. What I'm saying is this: I believe that having a regular time with the Lord will enhance your life. Hugely.

Our church's theme scripture is John 10:10. Copy the second part of that verse here:

"I have come that

_____

_____."

The **Message** reads, "I came so they can have real and eternal life, more and better life than they ever dreamed of."

If you could have a life that is "more and better than you could dream of" what would that look like?

_____

_____

_____

I saw a drama one Easter about the life of Jesus. One of the scenes in this play was so amazing that it sticks with me to this day.

Jesus and a crowd of people were on the stage when suddenly the spotlight rested on a man at the back of the auditorium. He slowly began to walk toward the front, coming down the center aisle. In his arms was a little girl who looked to be about 6 years old. This little girl had long brown hair. I remember it vividly because she way laying in his arms and her head was hanging all the way back. Her hair was hanging down halfway to the ground. The little girl was dead. Her body was totally lifeless. And this was her daddy. And he was slowly, sadly, with leaden steps, bringing her to Jesus.

As he approached the stage, where Jesus and the crowd was, all of the people in the crowd grew quiet and watched. Everyone saw Jesus turn, and this daddy placed his daughter's lifeless body into Jesus' arms. There was no conversation. None was needed. It was very clear what the father was asking Jesus to do.

Jesus took the little girl into his arms. She was completely lifeless, her head falling back, her long hair hanging down. He raised her up above His head until He was holding her high in the air with just His hands. And He looked up to heaven and prayed. His arms were extended over His head and this child was totally motionless…no life in her little body. She. Was. Dead.

After He prayed, Jesus started to lower her back into His arms, and when she got back about to the level of His chest, suddenly her head snapped up! And she looked at Him in the face! And then immediately she threw her arms around His neck and wrapped her legs around Him and hugged him with all of her might! And then, just as suddenly, she began squirming and kicking as if to say, "I want down, let me down!"

So Jesus, laughing, put her down on the ground, and the little girl started running-just like little girls do.

Of course the crowd reacted in amazement as the girl ran over to her daddy and threw herself into his arms. She hugged him for a minute, but not for long. She squirms away from him, too, and dashes around the stage, first around one group of people and then the next. The whole time everybody on the stage watched and laughed in amazement at this little girl, once dead, but now ALIVE! She's ALIVE! With LIFE! And she's excited about it! She's a little girl! Little girls are supposed to run! And they are supposed to be excited about life! And she is.

Before I saw this play—when I had read this story in the Bible—I would read it and imagine that the little girl was lying on a bed, and Jesus came in and touched her head and she just kind of sat up and shook her head a little bit as if to say, "Wow, that was weird." And her mama would come over to the bed and hug her and cry. But this play was so good at vividly showing the contrast between death, with her lifeless body in Jesus' arms, and then BOOM…LIFE! Squirming and running and jumping and hugging LIFE!

I believe *that's* what the Lord has for each of us: a life full of excitement and enthusiasm and excellence! And I believe as we come into God's presence, Jesus is the only One who has the power to infuse us with that kind of life. As we choose daily to have an appointment with Him, to connect with our Power Source, he gives us LIFE and LIFE more abundantly.

I sincerely hope that this study encourages you to set aside a specific part of your day for the Lord. I'm hoping that when your alarm goes off and you're thinking about hitting the snooze button, you'll remember the story of Granddaddy and Mark and you'll decide to get up and spend some time with God, because His friendship is worth it.

Or maybe in the middle of the day, when something bad happens and you are tempted to be angry with God for allowing it, I'm hoping you'll remember the difference between David's response and Obed-Edom's response to being near the ark of the covenant. And you'll choose to draw near to God's presence, not away from Him.

Or perhaps some night when you are worn out from the activity of the day, and ready to get in the bed, you'll remember the story of the little girl Jesus raised from the dead, and you'll remember He wants to give you abundant life. And you'll take a few minutes to connect with Him, so He can do that for you.

Whatever the case, my hope and prayer is that by doing this study with me, you will make sure somewhere in your day there are opportunities to spend some alone time with the Lord and His Word.

Day Ten

For years I've taught this: *"Thou shalt have a quiet time! Thou shalt get out of thy bed at an unbelievably early hour and gather thine books and notebooks and pens and journals and thou shalt study diligently until thy head swims"...* Or something like that.

However, what I'm beginning to see is that I've made this "quiet time" into what works for me! I love early mornings-- that's when I'm at my best. I love to read and write and study. It's the way God wired me. *But He wired us all differently.* (Interesting, that wired and weird are the exact same letters put together in a different order. If you're not wired like I am, doesn't that make you weird?) We are not created alike. Therefore, the way that we connect with God is not always going to look the same.

I read a book a while back about seven different "Spiritual Pathways". The author, John Ortberg, said that people are created to connect with God in different ways. We are not the same. (And we can just praise God for that, amen?) Let's take a look at these seven spiritual pathways you can consider which of the pathways seem to fit you best. Then, *do it.* Walk the spiritual pathways! Be with God. It will help you accept truth and reject lies. And that, my friend, is a worthwhile goal.

Ortberg writes:
Our individual uniqueness means we will all experience God's presence and learn to relate to him in different ways...God wants to be fully present with each of us. But because he made us to be different from one another, we are not identical in the activities and practices that will help us connect with him...A spiritual pathway has to do with the way we most naturally sense God's presence and experience spiritual growth.

He lists the following seven
"Spiritual Pathways":

Intellectual pathway – People with this kind of a pathway feel God's presence more as they learn more about Him. They like to read, they love books and words and studying. The apostle Paul probably connected to God in this way. He wrote to Timothy, "Study to show yourself approved unto God."

Acts 17:11 mentions a group of people who implemented this spiritual pathway: "Now the Bereans were of more noble character than the Thessalonians, for they received the message with great eagerness and examined the Scriptures every day to see if what Paul said was true."

I remember being at a bookstore, looking at a children's book together with a friend of mine. She was delighting in the illustrations of forests and animals and snow, and I was totally into the rhyme and flow of the words. Same book, different women, different pathways. Those with the intellectual pathway love great books, deep thoughts, and sound teaching.

Is the intellectual pathway a spiritual pathway you can relate to?

_____

–

Can you think of someone you know who tends toward an intellectual pathway?

_____

_____

Relational pathway – Folks with this pathway have a deep sense of God's presence when they are involved in significant relationships. These people have "their people." Remember "Welcome Back Kotter"? In the pilot episode when Mr. Kotter is meeting his students, Vinnie Barbarino motions to the rest of the class and says, (imagine this with a strong New York Italian accent) "My name is Vinnie Barbarino, and these are my people."

A person with this relational pathway loves small groups and visiting, sharing ideas and being with people. Ortberg writes,
People on this pathway need to lead a relationally rich life. They need to be part of friendships and small groups that are growing in depth and vulnerability. They will discover that they are much more likely to practice prayer or acts of servanthood when they can do it in a relational context.

It's quite possible that Jesus' disciple, Peter would have had this kind of a pathway. He was almost always involved in the small group including Peter, James, and John. Are you a relational person?

_____

Who do you know that would fit into this category?

_____

Serving Pathway - With these people, God's presence seems most tangible when they are helping others. They may feel uncomfortable when they don't have a job to do. When they are engaged in acts of service, they sense God's presence in their lives.

I was at a volunteer appreciation banquet one evening and a couple showed up early "to help." They routinely came to church events early to help set up. However, this time, they weren't allowed to help because the event was to honor them. They were the volunteers being appreciated! I could literally sense their discomfort as they were forced to simply sit down at a table and be waited on by the leadership. It was almost humorous. They just wanted to get up and serve! That's the way they felt close to God, by serving.

The New Testament talks about a woman named Dorcas who may have been wired this way. Acts 9 describes her as "always doing good and helping the poor." When this lady died, Peter showed up and, by the power of God, raised her from the dead! Dorcas was probably laying there dead thinking, "I don't have time to be dead, there are people to be served!"

Does serving others energize you?

_____

List the "serving" people in your life and thank the Lord for them:

_____

_____

Worship pathway – Yes, I can certainly relate to this one! These are the people who are excited to come to church so they can spend time in corporate worship services. They love celebration and expression. In worship they experience the reality of God's presence. They love to raise their hands or get on their knees, or other ways of outward expression of worship. King David was, without a doubt, one who experienced this way of connecting with God. Because of his "worship pathway," we have hundreds of Psalms with which to worship.

Do you fall into this category?

_____

Who do you know like this?

_____

_____

_____

Activist pathway – These people are looking for a cause; they have a passion to act, to do something. The people who immediately get in their trucks and head to the site of a natural disaster are definitely activist types. Challenges energize them. When someone says, "This can't be done," they smile and say, "Watch me!"

Nehemiah had an activist pathway. When he heard about how bad the city of Jerusalem had gotten, he felt compelled to go and do something about it.

Do you fall into this group of people?

_____

Who do you know with an activist pathway?

_____

_____

_____

Contemplative Pathway – If you have a contemplative pathway, you love large blocks of uninterrupted time alone. Reflection comes naturally to you. God is most present to you when distractions and noises are removed. If you get too busy, or spend too much time with too many people, you begin to feel drained and stretched thin. (Mothers of young children who have a contemplative bent may be in for a few years of frustration…they would benefit greatly from a night away occasionally, if at all possible.) I think of monks and nuns when I think of this pathway. The Apostle John may have been one of these, because he loved to bask in the adoration of God.

Are you contemplative?

_____

List the contemplatives in your life:

_____

_____

_____

Creation pathway - People like this love and appreciate the world God made. There is something deeply life-giving and God- breathed about nature for them. Being outside replenishes and energizes them. They see God in a waterfall or river or sunset or rainbow. Being out in creation opens their spirit to God. Jesus illustrated this pathway…and all of the others. He was constantly withdrawing from people to go up into the mountains or to be near a lake and commune with the Father.

Does being out in creation inspire you?

_____

List others you know who have this creation pathway:

_____

_____

_____

Ortberg writes: *Take a look through these descriptions, and try to assess which ones you most naturally follow. Make sure you incorporate practices that involve these pathways into the rhythms of your life…Celebrate that this is part of how God made you and wants to connect with you.*

This book impacted me and encouraged me to find additional ways to focus on the Lord, in addition to Bible study. He says that you may have more than one of these bents, in fact, you may enjoy several different ways of God-connection. However, don't take this as permission to simply try to "feel" close to the Lord. God has given us His Word as our primary source of communication with Him. Don't neglect the oh so very important pathway of Bible study, whether the intellectual pathway is part of your makeup or not. And whatever your other pathways are…do them! **On purpose!** With your whole heart! Seek God.

2 Chronicles 15:2 ~ the LORD is with you when you are with Him And if you seek Him, He will let you find Him.

Day Eleven

For some reason, we women tend to beat ourselves up for not being like someone else. As we discover the way God has individually created us, it's especially important not to compare ourselves to others. I can just imagine someone saying,

"Well, I guess I'm an intellectual, but I really wish that worship was the way I was bent." Or, "I like to serve others, and I know God is pleased when I do that, but I really wish I were better at reading books and writing in a journal. I just can't seem to stay committed to that."

I visited my sister, Jackie, in Chicago several years ago. While I was there, we drank a ton of Diet Coke. I remember standing in her kitchen watching as Jackie took the empty Coke box and began to open both ends. Then she folded the box flat and started tearing it into small pieces. I said, "What in the world are you doing?" She calmly replied, "I'm tearing down this box. Carl likes for me to do it this way." I was totally blown away! I said, "Good grief! Take the box. Throw it on the ground. Smash it till it's flat. And cram it in the garage trash can!" I couldn't believe the trouble she went to in order to have a tidy trash can!

A couple of weeks later I was home and had completed the consumption of 24 cans of Diet Coke. As I walked out to the garage to cram the box into the trash can this amazingly foreign thought crossed my mind. *"If I were really a good wife, I would tear this box into little pieces before I threw it away."* For just a half a minute I began to convince myself that **I wasn't a good wife** because of the state of my garage trash can!

I almost fell for it! I almost believed that thought!

Then, the next thought came—one that was more truth than lie. *"That's crazy! John doesn't care about my Coke boxes, he cares about where I park my car!"* I realized pretty quickly that what matters to one husband may or may not matter to another. Jackie's husband doesn't care about door dings on his cars; he wants tidy trash.

God used that moment to remind me **not to compare.** We don't need to be comparing ourselves to others. Not in the area of marriage, or careers, or giftings, or in the area of spiritual pathways. It's very important that you accept and embrace the way that God made you. Don't compare your spiritual pathway with somebody else's and wish that you were different! God knew exactly what He was doing when He created you, my friend!

God has created you with certain raw materials. He built into your personality likes and dislikes, and He did it on purpose! We are not clones, we are individuals created in His image. And He is multi-faceted and unique.

So rejoice in whatever your spiritual pathways are, and do them! Get with God! Connect with Him! Abide in Him! Let Him communicate with you. He wants that very much.

Let me be clear about this point, however. **The primary way the Lord communicates with us is through His word.** So even if your spiritual pathway leans toward connecting with God through a pathway other than the intellectual one, be sure you are also spending time in Bible reading and study! The Bible tells us in 2 Timothy 2:15,

Be diligent to present yourself approved to God, a worker who doesn't need to be ashamed, correctly teaching the word of truth.

Reading the Bible is the best way to hear from God.

We are probably all familiar with the verse in Jeremiah 29:11 that tells us that God knows the plans He has for us, plans for good and not evil. If you keep reading in that passage, you'll find this:

"You will seek Me and find Me when you search for Me with all your

heart." -- Jeremiah 29:13

This passage in the Message is especially beautiful:

'I know what I'm doing. I have it all planned out—plans to take care of you, not abandon you, plans to give you the future you hope for. When you call on me, when you come and pray to me, I'll listen. When you come looking for me, you'll find me. Yes, when you get serious about finding me and want it more than anything else, I'll make sure you won't be disappointed.' God's Decree.

God wants to have a relationship with us. The Bible shows us this reality from beginning to end.

We begin with the Old Testament, when God was trying to reveal Himself to mankind through the nation of Israel. In the Old Testament we read about priests and prophets and the Law and how God delivered Israel again and again.... ***God wanted to have a relationship with His people.***

As the Old Testament ends, the first four books of the New Testament are the gospels —when God actually became a human being and came down Himself to reach out to mankind. The gospels tell the story of how He came to show the world how very much He loves us. He demonstrated this love not only by walking on the earth and doing good while He was here, but by dying on the cross and giving his very life for every person. ***God wanted to have a relationship with His people.***

Following the gospels is the book of Acts—the Acts of the apostles. Then comes the epistles. These were stories of what happened in the early church. After Jesus ascended into Heaven, a small group of people, empowered by the Holy Spirit, began to spread the story of Jesus. The epistles tell how His story started this world-changing revolution. ***God wanted to have a relationship with His people!***

Now here's the cool thing…we are still making history! We are still in the age of the church and we have the opportunity to continue what the apostles started. We do this by following their example. They listened to the leading of the Holy Spirit and then obeyed. That's what we want to do—listen to God as He walks and talks with us. Ask Him to interrupt our lives with Holy Spirit experiences. The very best way to hear His voice is to read the Bible. *God still wants to have a relationship with His people, with YOU, in fact. God wants to have a relationship with YOU.*

He has wired you in such a way that you have this built-in pathway, this unique-to-you tendency toward a certain way of connecting with Him. You may be an intellectual, a studier…a contemplative, a thinker…a worshiper or relationally wired. You may love to get outside into creation to seek God…you may be a servant or an activist. Probably you are combination of many of these. Whatever you are, this is my encouragement to you today: **Do it**…**on purpose.** Figure out what your pathways are and then do them. Seek God. Seek God. Seek God. Look for Him until you find Him and then stay with Him for a while.

Every day do this.

Every day do this.

Do this every day.

Create your very own appointment with God. And keep it. He will meet you there.

"When you seek me, you shall find me, when you search for me with your whole heart."

"Yes, when you get serious about finding me and want it more than anything else, I'll make sure you won't be disappointed."

He will let Himself be found. He is longing for you to find Him in commonplace experiences.

Your only assignment today is this: Write a prayer to the Lord, expressing your desire to connect to Him. Include your plan for daily connecting with Him. Ask Him to help you be consistent in this goal.

_____

_____

_____

_____

_____

_____

_____

Day Twelve

When I was a teenager, I listened to music on what was called record albums. These were vinyl disks somewhat larger than today's cd's. (Well, yesterday's cd's...most of us download our music digitally these days...) At any rate, these record albums could get scratches on them and develop places where the music would skip. A word or two would be left out of the song. Of course, like all teenagers, I listened to these albums over and over again, ~~and~~ then over again. The songs became permanently imprinted on my brain.

I didn't realize how permanently until a few years ago. I found that some of the artists I had listened to as a teenager had rerecorded their music twenty-five years later. It was recorded on cd this time. Of course I had to own one! Listening to it, I realized an amazing thing. I still remember where my old record albums had skipped! In fact, when I sang along with those old songs, my brain skipped where my old albums had skipped. On the new cd, of course, there was no scratch; therefore all of the words were clear, but my brain remembered the skip.

Our brains are amazing things. After twenty -five years, still remembering something like that is incredible. But that's the way God has created us. If you do say something over and over and then over again, it can become so ingrained in your brain that you do it without thinking about it.

Imagine a big glob of jelly on a plate. Now imagine spooning hot water on top of that glob of jelly. The first spoonful you put on the jelly will create grooves and channels for the water to flow through. Then the next spoonfuls you pour on the jelly will follow those existing channels. The grooves will deepen and become more distinct as you add hot water. The more times you spoon water over the jelly, the deeper the channels become.

The mind will channel information that it receives in a similar way. What we receive conforms to the already existing configurations in our minds. The more we repeat something, or believe something, the more our brains accept that action, or word, or thought to be true. We develop thought patterns that become habits. So if we repeat it often enough, we can actually become convinced that it's true. Even if it's not.

If I had only listened to those albums a few times, I may not have remembered the places they skipped. But because I listened to them hundreds of times, that skip became indelible in my mind.

This concept would be a great thing if our words and thoughts are always positive and good, if we are thinking and saying truth. But if we are believing negative thoughts or lies, it is not such a good thing.

What if I said to myself over and over again, "We simply do not have enough income to pay these bills. We'll never be able to get out of debt. Our finances are a mess!"? Or what if I said, "That is the third time this week he's made a comment like that to me! He makes me so mad! I'm not sure this marriage is going to last. Surely there's something better than this! Maybe we should just go ahead and get a divorce."?

Write an example of a negative thought you are tempted to believe:

_____
_____
_____
_____

If we repeat these kinds of things to ourselves, they become entrenched in our brains. Then, even though they are lies, and are indeed false, we begin to believe that they are true. When we accept these lies as reality, they may actually come to pass. We don't have enough to pay the bills, or we do head toward a divorce.

We've got to stop this while it's still in the thought realm! We've got to make a choice to transform our minds by changing the way we think.

Look up Romans 12:2.

Rewrite this scripture in your own words:

_____
_____
_____
_____
_____

Now look up Romans 12:2 in The Message. What phrases jump out to you in this version?

_____

_____

_____

_____

The New Living Translation of this verse is, "Don't copy the behaviors and customs of this world, but let God transform you into a new person by changing the way you think."

God wants to change the way we think!

How in the world does that happen?

Consider this commentary quote:

*But refusing to conform to this world's values must go even deeper than the level of behavior and customs—it must go to the **transforming of the way we think**. Believers are to experience a complete transformation from the inside out. And **the change must begin in the mind**, where all thoughts and actions begin. Much of the work is done by God's Spirit in us, and **the tool most frequently used is God's word. As we memorize and meditate upon God's word, our way of thinking changes**. Our minds become first informed and then conformed to the pattern of God, the pattern for which we were originally designed. When believers have had their minds transformed and are becoming more like Christ, they will know what God wants and they will want to do it for it is good, pleasing to God, and perfect for them.*

Notice the phrase, **"The tool most frequently used is God's word."** The method we use to change the way we think is God's written word. We reject lies and believe the truth. The Bible is where we find the truth. Not in magazines or newspapers. Not on the Internet. Not on talk shows. Not even on the telephone with our best friend. The Bible is where we find the truth. The written word of God.

But look! Jesus said, "I am the way, <u>the truth</u> and the life". John 14:6

And look at this! "But when He, the <u>Spirit of truth</u> comes, He will guide you into <u>all truth</u>."

Wow! So the written word is truth, and Jesus is the truth, and the Holy Spirit is the Spirit of truth! Three different ways for us to find truth—different, yet very much the same. Scripture tells us that Jesus is the Word of God who came in the flesh. We also know that God the Father, Jesus, His Son, and the Holy Spirit are one. So it is through all three of these that we can find truth.

I point this out to you because I want you to see that it's not only through memorization and repetition of scriptures that our minds are changed. I do believe that it is important to know the Word, to memorize and quote scriptures. But also, equally important, maybe even *more* important is **having a relationship** with Jesus, as well as a **relationship with the Holy Spirit**, the Spirit of truth. Remember that **relationship** is what God wants. He wants us to spend time listening to His voice. He promises to whisper in our ears. And the truth that He whispers frequently is of His love for us.

In closing today, spend a few moments being quiet before the Lord. Ask Him what it is He would like to speak to you today. Then be still and listen. Recognize the presence of the Lord. Let Him pour into your heart whatever it is that He has for you today.

Respond to His words in prayer:

_____

_____

_____

_____

_____

_____

_____

_____

_____

_____

_____

_____

Metamorphosis of the Mind:
Experiencing Jesus as the Truth

Day Thirteen

Therefore, my brother, who would learn to abide in Jesus, take time each day, where you read, and while you read, and after you read, to put yourself into living contact with the living Jesus, to yield yourself distinctly and consciously to His blessed influence; so will you give Him the opportunity of taking hold of you, of drawing you and keeping you safe in His almighty life.

Andrew Murray

Yesterday we discussed repetition and how listening to something many times over causes it to become ingrained in our minds until we believe it as truth. We looked at Romans 12:2 where scripture encourages us to renew our minds by changing the way that we think.

The Bible is our only source of absolute truth. It is vital that we use God's Word as our sure answer to life's questions. It is also of utmost importance to connect with the Living Word, Jesus Christ, through the power of the Holy Spirit.

Read Acts 22:3-16

By whom was Paul trained?

_____

This was one of the greatest rabbis in Hebrew history.

In his zeal, what did Saul do to followers of the Way?

_____

_____

_____

Saul's direction was completely changed by his encounter with Jesus, the Living Word of God.

What two questions did Saul ask during this amazing experience?

_____

_____

_____

_____

Saul knew the written word of God. He was by his own admission, "...thoroughly trained in the law." Yet it wasn't until he collided with the Living Word, Jesus Christ, on that dusty road to Damascus, that Saul began to realize God's amazing will for his life.

Jon Courson writes:

He thought he was protecting God's honor as he went throughout an entire region tracking down heretics who called themselves Christians, pulling them out of their homes, putting them in chains, and carrying them off to be imprisoned, tortured, and killed. As he traveled down the road to Damascus on one such mission, the Lord intervened and straightened him out.

Cynthia Heald writes:

Paul did not think he needed freedom— his heritage and the law made him complete. But a monumental encounter on the road to Damascus dramatically changed Paul's mind and life. **Truth Himself confronted this Pharisee of the Pharisees***. When he was spiritually blind, he could not see the truth, but in his physical blindness he recognized and embraced the Truth, and he was set free.*

Saul knew the law. But he didn't know the Lord. He knew the rules, but he had no relationship. He had extraordinary zeal, but his zeal was misguided. He hadn't yet been properly introduced to the lover of his soul. After meeting Jesus, the One who would capture his heart, Saul became Paul, the writer of much of the New Testament. He became one whose love for Jesus far exceeded any fear he may have felt in the face of tribulation. He became the one who wrote,

"For me to live is Christ, and to die is gain." Philippians 1:21

Saul's second question was this, "What shall I do, Lord?" Jesus' response to Saul was to get up and go to Damascus. He said that Saul's next assignment would be given to him there.

After going to Damascus, Saul met Ananias, who said to him, "The God of our fathers has chosen you **to know his will**." I believe that you and I have also been chosen to know God's will. Scripture says that He is intimate with the upright. We are the righteousness of God in Christ, therefore, we are upright. God wants to be intimate with you! He wants to be intimate with me! I believe He wants very much for us to know His will. It's not a secret He is trying to keep from us. He wants us to know it, and as a result of our love for Him, I believe he wants us to do it.

Let's revisit Romans 12:2:

Do not conform any longer to the pattern of this world, but be transformed by the renewing of your mind. Then you will be able to test and approve <u>what God's will is—his good, pleasing and perfect will.</u>

What does this scripture say follows transformation by the renewal of our minds?

_____

Knowing His will!

Jon Courson writes,
The word translated 'prove' in Romans 12:2 is a word not of academics, but of intimacy—as in Genesis 4:1, where Scripture records that Adam 'knew' Eve. This doesn't mean Adam knew about Eve intellectually. It means he knew her intimately. And this is what Paul is declaring to us. You can know God's will intimately.

When Saul asked "What shall I do, Lord?" he was setting an example for you and me. This is a question we should be asking daily. *"What is it that You have for me to do today, Lord? How can I carry out Your will for my life this day?"* When we encounter and experience Truth, Himself, we begin to recognize His will for our lives— a will which includes our freedom.

True freedom is found in a vital, growing relationship with the Lord Jesus. Jesus (the Living Word of God) has revealed Himself in the Scripture (the written Word of God). If we want to know Him, if we want to know the Truth, we must devote ourselves to the reading, study, and meditation of His Word. There is no substitute and there are no shortcuts. The enemy is constantly confronting us with his lies. In order to combat his deception, our minds and hearts must be filled with the Lord Jesus and saturated with His Word. --- Nancy Leigh DeMoss

Pray with me now as we end today's lesson together:

Lord Jesus, I recognize that studying and knowing Your written Word is very important. That's why I'm doing this lesson right now. I know it will benefit me. I also know that You are the Living Word of God. I know that you are Truth. Therefore, I'm asking You now to reveal Yourself to me in a deeper way than ever before. Please be intimate with me. Please interrupt my life the way You interrupted Saul's. I want a relationship with You, not rules and religion. I'm giving You full permission to have Your way in my life. Let Your will be done, not mine. In Jesus' name...for Jesus' glory. Amen.

Metamorphosis of the Mind:
Experiencing Jesus as the Truth

Day Fourteen

Yesterday we talked about how both the written Word of God and Jesus, the Living Word of God are our sources for truth. Today we'll be looking at the exciting third Person of the Godhead.

Look up John 14:16 and 17

What will the Father give?

_____

_____

This Counselor is called the Spirit of _____.

The New Living Translation says, "He is the Holy Spirit, who leads into all truth." Cynthia Heald writes, "The Holy Spirit's ministry in our lives is profound, probably more significant than we can ever realize."

We are told that at creation, "The Spirit of God was hovering over the face of the waters." (Gen 1:2). Job proclaimed, "The Spirit of God has made me, and the breath of the Almighty gives me life" (Job 33:4). Jesus told Nicodemus, "That which is born of the flesh is flesh, and that which is born of the Spirit is spirit" (John 3:6); and to others He said, "It is the Spirit who gives life" (John 6:63). Jesus referred to the Holy Spirit as **the Spirit of truth**. The Holy Spirit is the **author of all truth**.

Wow! So we have the Bible…and we have Jesus…and we have the Holy Spirit! All three were given to us to help us find truth! According to John 16:13, not only is He called the Spirit of truth, but His purpose will be to:

_____

_____

_____

2 Thessalonians 2:13 says that we have been chosen to be saved through the sanctifying work of the Spirit and through belief_____ _____ _____.

Titus 1:1 tells us that the ____ _____ ____ _____ _____ leads to godliness.

One of the major goals of this study is for us to learn and believe truth. We see yesterday and today that God has given us His written Word, His Son, and His Spirit to help us accomplish this goal.

As you endeavor to spend time with the Lord— in your own personal devotions— I'm hoping that you will tap into all three of these sources in your search for truth. When I begin my quiet time each morning I pray and ask the Holy Spirit to be there. I ask Him to reveal Himself through the written Word. I welcome Jesus to interrupt my studying and show Himself to me.

Sometimes as part of my devotions, I take the written Word and put it into my own words. I change it into language that makes sense to me. The following is an example of this.

Psalm 19:7-11:

"The law of the Lord is perfect, reviving the soul."

The Bible is perfect, it has no flaw, no blemish, nothing wrong or false about it. When I read the Bible, it revives me. It stirs me up and gives me enthusiasm in my spiritual life.

"The statutes of the Lord are trustworthy, making wise the simple."

I know I can trust whatever the Bible says. It will make me wise, even though I'm just an ordinary person.

"The precepts of the Lord are right, giving joy to the heart."

The Bible is always right, and when I read it and do it, it will make my heart glad. I'll have true joy when I'm doing what it says.

"The commands of the Lord are radiant, giving light to the eyes."

The Bible sheds light on my path. Reading the Bible is one way that I can know God's will for my life.

The fear of the Lord is pure, enduring forever. The ordinances of the Lord are sure and altogether righteous."

Fearing the Lord results in purity that lasts forever. The Bible is completely trustworthy. Advice from the Bible doesn't change like advice you may find in newspapers or magazines.

"They are more precious than gold, than much pure gold; they are sweeter than honey, than honey from the comb."

The Bible is better than anything this world has to offer: money, material things, scrumptious foods. It's better than anything.

"By them is your servant warned; in keeping them there is great reward."

When I read the Bible, it gives me clear direction and helps me stay out of trouble. I know that obeying scriptural concepts will be of great benefit to me.

Doing this causes me to really look at what the passage is saying, rather than just reading a few chapters so I can say that I have done my Bible reading. I believe that the time we spend with the Lord can be **interactive.** He wants it to be! Please don't allow it to be routine or ordinary. God wants to interrupt you just as surely as He interrupted Saul on the road to Damascus! His plan is for you and I to be as effective in our own circles of influence as Paul was in the early church. I truly believe that.

Please pick out a favorite passage and put it into your own words.   Call it "The Message, according to _____ (your name)":

_____

_____
_____
_____
_____
_____
_____
_____
_____

_____

_____

_____

_____

_____

_____

_____

_____

_____

_____

_____

_____

_____

_____

_____

_____

Ain't it fun?

Metamorphosis of the Mind:
Experiencing Jesus as the Truth

Day Fifteen

It was the first day of school, so I told the students a little bit about myself. I told them where I was born, about my family, what sort of things I enjoy, general stuff like that. On the last day of that week, I asked them to recall facts I had told them five days earlier.

Mrs. Hewitt: *"So, what do you know about me?"*
Student: *"You were born in Pensacola!"*

Me: *"Yep, that's right, and what do I like there?"*
Student: *"You like the beach and the naval air museum."*

Me: *"Yep, what else do you know about me?"*
Student: *"You're Maggie and Phillip's mom."*

Me: *"That's right, what about pets?"*
Student: *"You have a cat named Sydney."*

Me: *"Yes, that's all correct. Those are all things I told you last Monday. You may even know other things, things that we didn't talk about on Monday. But...do you really know me? You know some facts about me, I know some facts about you, but do we really know each other? If not, how can we get to know each other?"*

We discussed that in order to get to know each other, we would have to spend time together. I told them that I might invite them to my office, and if I did, not to worry. You're not always in trouble when you get invited to the principal's office. In fact, this principal keeps a candy jar on her bookshelf!

Our discussion continued. I asked if they knew any facts about Jesus. They knew a lot. After all, these kids had been in Christian school for a long time. Then I asked, "But do you really *know* Him?" We talked about knowing Jesus, about how that would be the theme of our entire school year:"Knowing You, Jesus."

"What is more, I consider everything a loss compared to the surpassing greatness of knowing Christ Jesus my Lord."
Philippians 3:8
"Let us know, let us press on to know the Lord." Hosea 6:3

"Now this is eternal life: that they may know You, the only true God, and Jesus Christ, whom You have sent." John 17:3

So we're studying now about renewing our minds. We're talking about how to recognize lies and reject them, about how to believe truth. When we recognize that a thought we have is untrue, we'll find that scripture often exposes that lie. Meditating on these scriptures will help us begin to believe the truth of God's Word instead of the lie.

But what I'm beginning to see is that it will take more than just a mental assent. A cognitive agreement that God's Word is truth is not enough to lead us to a victorious life. A relationship with the Lord is what brings about victorious living. That's why it's so very cool that Jesus is the Living Word and the Holy Spirit is the Spirit of Truth— because they are *individuals we can know*. They are Beings that *we can have a relationship* with. So, we need to do more than just memorize verses. We need to build relationships! This is about knowing Jesus! (And the way that's going to happen is by going to His office, by spending time with Him, a.k.a. a daily quiet time.)

Our goal is to **experience Jesus as the Truth**. When we experience Him, and allow Him to touch our emotions with His very presence, then the truth will stick. It will be a "learning" that lasts. This is more than rote memory and repetition…it comes from a love relationship.

Think about people you love. Think about your parents, siblings, husband, children, friends. We are involved with our loved ones on many different levels. We enjoy their personalities, we spend time serving them, we laugh together, cry together, snuggle with them. We *experience life* with those whom we love. Jesus wants us to do that with Him, too. As we experience Jesus, His truth will permeate our minds and change the way we think.

When I started writing this study, I knew that it would be based on two scriptures: the one about renewing our minds and the one about bringing every thought captive to Jesus. What I didn't know was the complete verse in 2 Corinthians. I was only remembering one phrase—the part about bringing every thought captive to Jesus. However, I looked it up and was surprised by what it says in its entirety!

Look up 2 Corinthians 10:5 in the NIV and fill in the phrases:

We demolish arguments and every pretension that sets itself up against ___ _____

__ ____ and we take captive _____ _____ to make it obedient to Christ.

--2 Corinthians 10:5

This scripture says that any thought we have that opposes **the knowledge of God** must be addressed. Knowing God! That's our goal! Anything that doesn't line up with knowing Jesus is not a thought we should be thinking. Wow...I didn't remember that part of the verse.

In the Garden of Eden, Adam and Eve had an amazing relationship with God. They walked together in the cool of the evening and enjoyed each other's company. They knew God. But that easy fellowship was destroyed when Eve believed the lie of the enemy, "If you eat this, you'll be like God." As a result of sin, Adam and Eve's friendship with God was destroyed. They were forced to leave the place where they had experienced God.

However, that was all changed when Jesus came. He came to provide reconciliation! He came to make things right between God and man. He came to rebuild the friendship that the lying snake had destroyed.

Romans 5:10 and 11 says:

For if, when we were God's enemies, we were reconciled to him through the death of his Son, how much more, having been reconciled, shall we be saved through his life! Not only is this so, but we also rejoice in God through our Lord Jesus Christ, through whom we have now received reconciliation.

Look this up in the New Living Translation and fill in the blanks: (Use your Scripture Index)

10 For since _____ _____ _____ _____ was restored by the death of his Son while we were still his enemies, we will certainly be saved through the

60

life of his Son. 11 So now we can rejoice in our wonderful new relationship with God because our Lord Jesus Christ has made us _____ ____ _____.

Now look up 2 Corinthians 5:17-19 in the NIV and fill in the blanks:

17 Therefore, if anyone is in Christ, he is a new creation; the old has gone, the new has come! 18 All this is from God, who_____ _____ _____

_____ through _____ and gave us the ministry of reconciliation: that God was reconciling the world to himself in Christ, not counting men's sins against them. And he has committed to us the message of _____.

Reconcile means "to re-establish fellowship between." That's what Jesus did when He came and gave His life for us. He re-established the fellowship that had been lost because of sin.

Do you know Him? Write a prayer of thanksgiving for the reconciliation He's provided. If you are feeling separated from God because of sin, confess that sin now and be reconciled to Him!

_____
_____
_____
_____
_____
_____
_____

Day Sixteen

Unless you demand it to be otherwise, your self-talk will tend to be negative. I'm not sure I understand why, but that's just the case. We are more likely to mutter under our breath something like "I am such an idiot" than "I am fearfully and wonderfully made."

Things I may say to myself include:

I'm unworthy.
I'm such an idiot.
I am insignificant.
I am a has-been.
I'm undisciplined.
I'm addicted.
My children don't need me.
I'm old.
Not as smart as I used to be.

Recently I met with a group of teenaged girls. As an icebreaker I asked them to make a list of words that described themselves. Then they traced their hand and wrote those descriptive words around the drawing of their hands. The words they wrote were mostly positive. It was an unspoken understanding that what I wanted them to do was find positive ways to describe themselves.

But this morning I'm thinking about ways I talk to myself when no one else is listening. If I created a hand outline with those secret thoughts today, my hand would be surrounded by words like: loser, failure, old lady, a fun old lady, but old and unfit nonetheless.

Unless you demand it to be otherwise, your self-talk will tend to be negative.

Unless you demand it to be otherwise.

Unless you are intentional.

Unless you discipline yourself to be in control of your thought life, the thoughts you have about yourself will tend to be negative.

Scripture tells us not to conform to this world, but to be transformed by the renewing of our minds. And it tells us how to renew our minds—by the cleansing of the washing with water through the Word.

So instead of believing myself when I have these secret thoughts, what would happen if I would replace them with the truth of God's Word?

Look up Philippians 1:6 NIV and complete:

Being confident of this, that he who_____ a _____ _____ in you will carry it on to _____ until the day of Christ Jesus.

Look up Jeremiah 29:11 NIV and complete:

For I know the _____ I have for _____," declares the LORD, "plans to _____ _____ and not to harm you, plans to give you _____ and a _____.

Look up 2 Peter 1:3 and complete:

His divine power has given us _____ ____ _____ for life and godliness through our _____ ____ _____ who called us by his own glory and goodness.

If I replaced my negative thoughts with these truths from the Bible, I suspect what would happen is that I would begin to believe the Word and reject the lies. But to do this takes effort. It's not something that is just going to happen. My tendency, for some reason, can be to believe the negative thoughts. To beat myself up. To agonize over past failures. To live in defeat.

Perhaps the reason is because we have an adversary, an enemy, the devil, who is seeking to devour us. He wants us to live this way. Scripture tells us he is the prince of the power of the air. He rules much of the world in which we live, and his influences are everywhere in our culture.

I'm not always negative. Sometimes my tendency is to be encouraged and encouraging rather than discouraged. But sometimes...well, sometimes I just get bummed out. And I may or may not have a good reason! Sometimes there is no reason at all. Regardless of the cause of my funk, here's the deal: It will take effort to change. I have to purpose to do it. It doesn't just happen by itself. I have to change my self-talk.

This is something I can't do in my own strength. I've got to have help to make this happen. That's where the Holy Spirit comes in:
- o Scripture says He's our Teacher.
- o Scripture says He's our Helper.
- o Scripture says He "comes alongside to help."

Look up John 14:26 and fill in the blanks:

But the Helper, the Holy Spirit, whom the Father will send in My name, He will _____ you all things, and _____ ____ ___ _____ ____

_____ _____ ____ _____.

Look up John 15:26 and complete:

"When the _____ comes, whom I will send to you from the Father, that is the _____ ____ _____ who proceeds from the Father, He will testify about Me.

Cry out to Him! Ask Him for help! Recognize His presence and take advantage of it. He wants to help you. He wants to remind you of the truth.

Let's take a look at just a couple of the lies I tell myself and see how they line up with scripture:

Lie- "I will never change. I will always be a loser."
Truth says: "Yup, you will never change ...as long as you are depending on yourself to make change happen." Jesus said, "Apart from Me, you can do nothing."

But Scripture also says, *"He who began a good work in you will perfect it."* **God doesn't ask us to pull ourselves up by the bootstraps!** He doesn't require us to be self-made women. In fact, He makes it very clear that we need His help to change. Our fleshly nature wars against our spiritual nature. We need the power of God to change.

Look up Romans 8:11 and complete:

And if the _____ __ _____ _____ _____ _____ _____ _____ _____ is living in you, he who raised Christ from the dead will also give life to your mortal bodies through his Spirit, who _____ ____ _____.

Wow, look at what's been given to us through Jesus. "That same Spirit that raised Christ from the dead dwells in you." That same power that was behind Jesus' resurrection is available to us! In fact, scripture says it lives in us!

Jesus was beaten to the point of being unrecognizable as a human being. Then He was hung on a cross until He died. He was then brought back to life by the power of this Spirit. If that Spirit's power is available to me, then my struggle against sin is not hopeless. **Change is possible through the power of the Holy Spirit.**

Lie- *"I'm such a bonehead/idiot.* (Fill in the blank with your favorite derogatory name.)

Usually when I say this to myself it's because I have done something or said something that I wish I hadn't done or said. The cool thing about knowing God is this; when we do or say something we shouldn't (when we sin), there is a way to have that sin forgiven. Many times when I say, *"I'm such an idiot"* what I really should be saying is, *"Jesus, I really blew it in that situation, will you please forgive me?"* And then, if necessary, I may need to go to a person and ask the same thing.

Truth says, *"If we confess our sins, He is faithful and righteous to forgive us our sins and to cleanse us from all unrighteousness."* 1 John 1:9

The truth of scripture also instructs us as believers to forgive each other when necessary. Fill in the blanks using your scripture index from Ephesian 4:32.

And be kind and compassionate to one another, _____ _____ _____, just as God also forgave you in Christ.

See how this works? If we recognize what's happening—that we recognize we are believing lies— and then chose to replace those lies with the truth of God's Word, we can change the way we think.

What lie are you commonly tempted to believe?

_____

_____

_____

_____

What scriptures can you find that address this issue?

_____

_____

_____

_____

_____

End today's session by asking the Lord to help you quickly recognize when you are believing a lie. That's the first step (and sometimes the trickiest part...).

Metamorphosis of the Mind:
Experiencing Jesus as the Truth

Day Seventeen

Have you ever been driving down the street, minding your own business, when a car pulls up next to you with music blasting so loudly that your whole vehicle vibrates? Doesn't that just burn you up? Man! Who died and made them king of the airways, right??? I mean, I like loud music, but only when it's MY loud music, know what I mean?

Whatever is loudest is easiest to hear.

We've already established that in this culture we are surrounded by lies. Blasting into our consciousness without being invited. We also know that God is everywhere. We can see Him in His creation. We can find him in His Word. We hear His voice when we talk to other believers.

So I guess the question is this: What will we choose to hear?

The lies may sound louder than the truth; they compete with a vengeance; they are more blatant and flagrant. But we have to search for the truth. It's quieter and we have to look for it. *We must discipline ourselves to focus on truth and reject lies.* It's a discipline that requires effort. It's not going to just happen. We must purpose in our hearts with all our strength to believe truth. Daily immersing ourselves in the Bible will make truth louder than lies.

Beth Moore calls it **"being *deliberate* about abandoning the lie."** She says lies lead us to specific actions, and if we want to change our behavior, we must change the underlying motives and attitudes that lead to those behaviors. To change attitudes of the heart that are wrong, we must first abandon the lies we're believing. We can ask God to identify the lie. This is why knowing Him, why having an intimate relationship with Him is so important. Spending time in the Word is the best way to have an intimate relationship with Him.

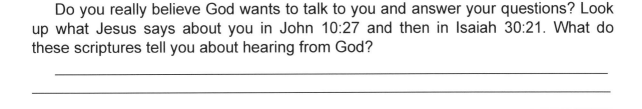

Do you really believe God wants to talk to you and answer your questions? Look up what Jesus says about you in John 10:27 and then in Isaiah 30:21. What do these scriptures tell you about hearing from God?

_____

_____

_____

_____

We can be confident that when we ask God to show us something, He will. He wants us to relate to Him in this way. We ask, and He answers in that still small voice of His Holy Spirit. Try Him in this. He may not speak to you in an audible voice, in fact, He probably won't. But He has a way of giving us an understanding down in our spirit of what He wants us to know. It might take some practice to begin to hear His voice, but ask Him to teach you, I believe that He will. He'll show Himself to be faithful to you. Remember that His voice will always be in agreement with the Bible.

Renewing my mind with God's Word is a discipline, something I must make myself do. For some reason it is easier to beat myself up with condemnation than to remind myself of the truth. I wonder why that is…

What happens is this: I blow it in some way. I mess up and do something that I know isn't pleasing to the Lord. From here a couple of different things may happen. I either go into denial and refuse to admit I'm sinning, or else I know it, recognize it, and just keep going in it! It's the craziest thing!

The apostle Paul finds himself in a similar state when he writes: "I do not understand what I do," (How many of you have ever felt that way?!) "For what I want to do, I do not do, but what I hate, I do…for I have the desire to do what is good, but I cannot carry it out." Romans 7:15, 18

So I blow it and, then for some unknown reason, I continue in it for a while. And I'm miserable in it. But I keep on! Either I keep on sinning or I spend my energy agonizing over the fact that I have been sinning—that I've blown it again. (Like that's any surprise…of course I've blown it. I'm still human. I'm still this side of heaven…yes, Virginia, you will sin while on this earth.) So, why don't I just recognize it, confess it, and be rid of the condemnation that inevitably follows? Why does there have to be this period of time when I beat myself up? I suggest that is simply part of Satan's plan. If he can keep us wallowing in guilt and condemnation, we will not be accomplishing anything for the kingdom of God. He wants us to wallow and moan and groan and agonize and become paralyzed by our shame at our own inability to overcome sin.

Here's truth: **We cannot overcome sin on our own.**

So I wonder what would happen if we simply agree with him? What if we say, "Yup, Satan, you're right, I have no power to stop this behavior in my own strength. Yes, I blew it again. But that's all the more reason for me to give praise to God, because He sent Jesus to pay the price for that very sin. And that sin…yes, the sin I just committed…that sin was nailed to the cross and therefore forgiven." And then we forget it and go on!

What if we actually did that? We agree with Satan when he accuses us. We confess that sin, recognize Jesus paid for it, therefore we're forgiven, and we go on with our life in grateful praise for the loving God we serve? Wouldn't that be so much easier than carrying around guilt, shame and condemnation and allowing it to wear us down?

Look up Romans 8:1. Because this is a very familiar scripture, there are several translations for you in your scripture index.

Write out your favorite translation here:

_____

_____

_____

_____

The word condemnation in the Greek is katakrima, meaning "*a decision* against someone, a condemnatory judgment."

A decision! A choice! When we walk around carrying a load of guilt and shame, we are making a choice, making a decision against ourselves.

My daughter Maggie lost her scooter. I remembered the last time she used it we had taken it to a park. Thinking we had left it in the trunk of a car downstairs, I went to the basement garage to try to find it. Our basement garage door is very near the woods behind our house. Sometimes snakes find their way into that lower garage.

I don't like snakes. At all.

So I'm walking downstairs into this dark, cold basement thinking about snakes. It was not fun. When I saw a coil of rope lying on the floor I jumped away like a crazy woman!

Right about the time my heartbeat was slowing, I remembered what I had been teaching my Bible Study friends. I remembered we have a choice about what we are thinking. So…. I changed my mind. I changed my thoughts. I decided, on purpose, deliberately, to think about Maggie playing outside in the sunshine on her scooter. Guess what? I was no longer worried about snakes. It works!

I'm telling you ladies, we can decide what we want to think about. We can decide to believe Satan when he speaks condemnation over us, or we can decide to believe God when He says we're forgiven. It's a choice. We get to decide. It can be as simple as that.

Rick Warren calls this 'the principle of replacement.' He says, "Turn your attention to something else. Don't fight the thought, just change the channel of your mind and get interested in another idea. This is the first step in defeating temptation."

Scripture tells us in Philippians 4:8 what we should think about.

Fix your thoughts on what is true, and honorable, and right, and pure, and lovely, and admirable. Think about things that are excellent and worthy of praise. Philippians 4:8 NLT

Let's close today by looking up one more scripture. Look up Romans 12:21 and copy it here:

_____

_____

_____

_____

How does this scripture relate to changing the way that we think?

_____

_____

_____

Pray that God will interrupt you today if you begin to believe lies. Ask Him to identify the lies for you. Then, ask Him for the strength and wisdom you will need to change the channel of your mind from lies to truth.

Day Eighteen

Yesterday we came to the conclusion that we are the ones who decide what we think about. It is a choice, merely a decision. We can change the channels in our minds and choose what to believe. That, my friends, is an amazing thing. We have power over our thought lives! We are not bound or obligated to certain thoughts.

Today I'd like to suggest that this not only applies to thoughts, but to feelings as well. A common lie believed by many people is this: ***My circumstances control my moods.*** In other words, if things are going well for me, I am happy and content. However, if life is full of hardships, I have to be angry, upset, and discouraged. What a lie! This is not true at all. It's not true and it's not Biblical either. It's simply a lie from the pit of hell. But, nevertheless, a lie many people believe and live out.

I once read a book called The Traveler's Gift. The main character in this story, David Ponder, is in the middle of tremendous struggles in his life. The book is about his experience of traveling back in time and visiting with significant historical figures. Each of these characters gives the "traveler" a gift of advice that will eventually change his life.
My favorite part of the book was when David Ponder visited with Anne Frank.

As you may remember, Anne Frank was a young Jewish girl who was forced into hiding during World War 2. They hid in an attic for several months. At this time, the Germans were kidnapping Jews and sending them off to concentration camps. There were also other families living in this attic at the time and the living conditions were brutal. Each person was required to remain perfectly still during the daytime. Otherwise, they might have been discovered by German soldiers. There was limited space and little food for several people. Anne's circumstances were horrible, and yet she had an attitude of thankfulness.

When David Ponder asks Anne about her rough conditions, Anne replies,

I do not complain. Papa says complaining is an activity just as jumping rope or listening to the radio is an activity. One may choose to turn on the radio, and one may choose not to turn on the radio. One may choose to complain, and one may choose not to complain. I choose not to complain.

Imagine that! Living in a small space for over a year with seven other people. She never left the attic. She kept perfectly still throughout the day, and was only able to move around at nighttime. And yet Anne chose to be happy. Although one of the women in that attic was a chronic complainer, Anne was determined to be content.

Her response to David Ponder continued, *"Our very lives are fashioned by choice, Mr. Ponder. First we make choices. Then our choices make us…an ungrateful person might see this place as too small for eight people, a diet that is limited and portions that are too meager, or only three dresses for two girls to share. But gratefulness is also a choice; I see an annex that hides eight people while others are being herded onto railway cars. I see food that is generously provided by Miep, whose family uses their ration cards for us. I see an extra dress for my sister and me while there are surely others who have nothing. I choose to be grateful. I choose not to complain."*

Wow…what amazing wisdom for such a young girl. Although the book, The Traveler's Gift, is a work of fiction, these comments were taken from a non-fiction work, The Diary of Anne Frank. There really was a young teenaged girl who believed these things.
Wouldn't it be great to have an attitude like that? It's merely a choice, my friends. Our moods are determined by simply making up our minds.

Let's turn our thoughts toward Paul and Silas in Philippi. They are involved in some very difficult circumstances, and yet their response is surprising. Read Acts 16: 16-34. What an amazing thing! These two men have been dragged through town by an angry crowd, stripped and beaten severely. Afterwards they were flogged and thrown into prison with their feet fastened in stocks. And yet, in the very middle of these horrific circumstances, scripture records an amazing thing.

Look at verse 25 and complete: About midnight Paul and Silas were

_____ and _____ _____ to God, and the other

prisoners were listening to them.

Are they allowing their current situations to control their moods? I don't think so. I think they are purposefully choosing to rejoice even in this terrible condition. I think they know something we may not have figured out yet. I think Paul and Silas realize this: **We act our way into feeling; we don't feel our way into acting.**

Undoubtedly Paul and Silas feel like moaning and groaning, and yet they're singing praises to God. Why? I wonder if they recognize that God is sovereign. I wonder if they know that He is not surprised by their situation. I wonder if they have the faith to believe that He will take their current situation and use it, not only for their own good, but also for the good of others.

The rest of the story reveals who benefits the most from their commitment to rejoicing. Who do you think benefits the most?

_____

How do Paul and Silas benefit as well?

_____
_____
_____

I believe when we choose to rejoice in harsh situations, not only is it good for us, but it is also good for those around us. That common phrase "If mama ain't happy, ain't nobody happy" has some truth to it. Your family will experience more joy, my friends, if you choose encouragement rather than discouragement. Paul and Silas realized they had a choice. And they chose to rejoice.

It's interesting to me that it is the Philippians, people who had become Christians that very night, to whom Paul later writes the instructions in Philippians 4:4.

Copy Phil 4:4 here:

_____
_____

Paul, in fact, gives this instruction to the Philippians three different times. Read Philippians 2:18 and 3:1. Three times Paul exhorts the Philippians to join him in his choice to rejoice.

Jon Courson writes:

*We are not commanded to rejoice **in our circumstances**, be they good or bad. No, we're to **rejoice in the Lord**. My circumstances may be bleak and brutal. But the Lord stands with me in those circumstances, and He will cause something good to come from them ultimately.*

Ladies, we are in control of our mood swings. We do not have to succumb to bad moods and irritability. Our current circumstances do not have to determine how we feel. We can choose how to feel. Paul did it...so can we.

"More than anything else, I believe it's our decisions, not the conditions of our lives, that determine our destiny."
  -Anthony Robbins

Metamorphosis of the Mind:
Experiencing Jesus as the Truth

Day Nineteen

Yesterday I quoted out of Jon Courson's Application Commentary of the New Testament: We are not commanded to rejoice in our circumstances, be they good or bad. No, we're to rejoice *in the Lord*. My circumstances may be crummy. But the Lord stands with me in those circumstances, and He will ultimately cause something good to come from them.

We can rejoice even when our **circumstances** are not good because **our God is good.** We rejoice "in the Lord." It's Him we are excited about. We can rest and rejoice in His character. Because our God is a good God and has promised to cause good things to come from all of our experiences, we can find joy.

Look up Philippians 1:12. Here Paul recognizes that although his circumstances have been brutal, good has come from them. In the NAS Version, this scripture says, "Now I want you to know, brethren, that my circumstances have turned out for the greater progress of the gospel."

Life is really hard right now, my circumstances stink…and you're telling me I need to rejoice? I don't think so.

Look it up in the NIV and copy it here:

_____

_____

_____

Continue reading through verse 14. What is the result of Paul having been in chains?

_____

_____

_____

Paul is going through a hard time. While he is writing this letter to the Philippians, he is in prison. He's bound with chains in a Roman jail! And yet, instead of whining and complaining, Paul is saying, "Hey, these good things have happened because of my chains."

Many times we are so focused on our own bad situations that we can't see anything good. All we can see is the crummy stuff happening to us. Yet even in the middle of these struggles, God promises that He'll use the hard times to make us grow.

Let's look at a very familiar verse together. Look up Romans 8:28 and copy it here:

_____

_____

_____

The Message version translates the verse this way:"That's why we can be so sure that every detail in our lives of love for God is worked into something good."

Every detail is worked into something good!

Every detail!

Every single detail!

Every joy, every disappointment, every accomplishment, every anxiety…everything.

Wow…how amazing. Our God is an amazing God.

My favorite Bible character (besides Jesus) might have to be Joseph.

Joseph was a guy who had lots of bad happen to him, but over and over again the scripture says, "But the Lord was with Joseph." Repeatedly Joseph has reasons to whine and complain or become bitter, but he doesn't! And so, time and again, God raises Joseph up to a leadership position.

You can read his inspiring story in Genesis chapters 37 and 39- 50. At the conclusion of this story, Joseph's brothers are afraid that he will exact revenge on them since their father has died. They fear retribution for the evil things they had done to him. But instead of paying them back for all they have done, Joseph makes a statement that illustrates the concept we are studying today.

Look up Genesis 50:20 and fill in the blanks. "You intended to harm me, but God

_____ ____ _____ _____, to accomplish what is now being done, the saving of

many lives."

When we begin to understand that **God's intention is always for our good**, our whining and complaining will lessen.

What do you tend to whine and complain about?

_____

_____

_____

_____

How could God use that situation for your good?

_____

_____

_____

_____

I would like to encourage you that God has a plan, and it's for your good! He's promised that in Jeremiah 29:11. Look it up in the NIV.

This is how it's paraphrased in the Message: "I know what I'm doing. I have it all planned out—plans to take care of you, not abandon you, plans to give you the future you hope for."

God knows what He's doing and He doesn't make mistakes. God never says "oops." Whatever your situation is, it is no surprise to God.

When I was growing up in Alabama, there was this southern expression that people said when they were frustrated. It was something they'd say as an exclamation, "God knows!" When I was really little and I'd hear someone say, "God knows," I thought they were actually talking about God's nose, and I would imagine this huge profile of God in the sky…God's great big nose floating among the clouds! Later I found out that's not what that meant at all.

Today that phrase means so much to me.
God knows…
Before I know…
God knows.
Even before it happens…
God knows.

He is not surprised!

He never says, "Oh, man! I wish I had remembered to...." He knows exactly what He's doing and He does it on purpose.

He does it on purpose. God purposefully works in our lives for our good.

So whatever it is in your life today, my friend... whether you're thinking about someone else or your own self, I would encourage you to trust your Creator. He will do what He has promised. He will work it out in such a way that you benefit. He will work it out for your good. It may take some time...but trust Him. He knows what He is doing.

Close by writing out a prayer of trust. Lay down your concerns and leave them in His hands.

_____

_____

_____

_____

_____

_____

_____

_____

_____

_____

_____

_____

_____

Day Twenty

When I was in college at Kansas State University, I shared a room with my friend, Bun. As most dorm rooms are, ours was decorated with posters and photos and such. I had a poster on my closet door that I had created with poster paper and crayons. I colored in huge artistic letters "COUNT IT ALL JOY." At the bottom of the page I finished out the scripture from James 1 in smaller letters…"knowing that the testing of your faith produces endurance."

It hung there from the beginning of the semester through the end of the year.

One day I came home from class feeling pretty disgusted about a particular grade I had just received. As soon as I walked in the door I began to complain to Bun. "I can't believe that professor gave me that grade! I know I deserved better than that! She just has no idea how long that project took." As I continued to bellyache about this grade, Bun quietly walked over to the closet door and began to take my poster down. I stopped long enough to look at her incredulously and ask, "What are you doing?"

She said, "I'm taking it down! It doesn't work!"

I stopped complaining.

We're still looking at the lie that is commonly believed and very easy to fall into: **My circumstances control my moods.** Another way to say this would be **I can only be happy when things are going my way.** This belief is contrary to the teachings of Christianity. The apostle Paul gave very clear instructions concerning how we are to respond when things don't go our way. He says we are to be joyful! To be happy when hard stuff comes…hmmm…that's pretty much the opposite of how my flesh wants to react.

Look up James 1:2 in the King James. Then look it up in the NIV. Notice any differences? What is the most significant difference between these two translations?

What is written as "temptations" in the KJV is translated "trials" in the NIV. The Greek word for both 'trial' and 'temptation' is the same.

Jon Courson explains,

*You see, what God will send or allow as a trial to strengthen our faith, Satan will seek to exploit to get us to sin. Conversely, what Satan throws our way as a temptation, God allows to be a trial. Satan wants to use the event to tear us down and wipe us out; God wants to use the same event to show us **how faithful He is and how real He can be.***

This passage continues in verses 3 and 4: ".... because you know that the testing of your faith develops perseverance. Perseverance must finish its work so that you may be mature and complete, not lacking anything."

Our Heavenly Father knows that as we endure hard situations, we grow and develop. We see "*how faithful He is and how real He can be.*" As we experience God's faithfulness, we mature and become changed more into the image of Christ.

Becoming more like Jesus is our goal as believers. Look up Romans 8:29 in the NIV and fill in the blanks:

29 For those God foreknew he also predestined to be _____ _____ _____ _____ ____ _____ _____, that he might be the firstborn among many brothers.

That phrase is translated in the New Living simply "to become like His Son."

Look up 2 Corinthians 3:18 in the NIV and fill in the blanks:

And we, who with unveiled faces all reflect the Lord's glory, _____ _____ _____ _____ _____ _____ with ever-increasing glory, which comes from the Lord, who is the Spirit.

The New Living says this:

So all of us who have had that veil removed can see and reflect the glory of the Lord. And the Lord—who is the Spirit—makes us more and more like him as we are changed into his glorious image.

We want to become like Jesus. That is our ultimate goal, to be changed into His image. God allows trials in our lives to make that happen.

Going through trials can push us into a closer relationship with God. When we are hurting, we learn the best way to find comfort is to run to our loving Father... Like a child who runs to Daddy when she's hurting or scared. When we struggle, we snuggle....true? Could be... Should be...ought to be. Instead of becoming frustrated and irritable or discouraged and depressed when times get tough, let your trials force you into the arms of your God.

Concerning a hard season she was experiencing in her life, Cheri Fuller writes:

*As I praised God, that deep heaviness began to lift and with it my anxiety about our stack of unpaid bills. It was as if dark glasses were removed and I saw what I'd never seen before: that no matter how difficult our situation was and even if nothing external changed, I could praise and thank God because **the trial would only draw me into a closer relationship with him.*** (Cheri Fuller~ Fearless: Building a Faith that Overcomes Your Fear).

Have you ever noticed the more time you spend with people, the more you become like them? Have you ever realized how we pick up common phrases, mannerisms, and styles of those we hang out with? By the same token, as we hang out with God, we become more like Him. Having an honest and real relationship with God encourages us to become transformed into the image of Christ.

So...is it a trial or a temptation? Perhaps there's a key here that will help us "count it all joy." If we see our current situations as trials—as an opportunity to grow, our response will be to press into Him. We will run to Him for comfort and assurance. If we see it as temptation coming from Satan, hopefully our response will be one of indignation. *"I certainly don't want to cooperate with him...no way am I falling for that one!"*

What do you do when you know you are being tempted by Satan?

_____

_____

_____

Read Matthew 4:1-11. What did Jesus do when Satan tempted Him?

_____

_____

_____   _____

Use the Word of God, friends. It is a powerful weapon against our enemy!

So, regardless of how you see the situation, whether you see it as a trial or a temptation, our goal is to not allow our emotions to be ruled by our circumstances. We want to overcome our fleshly tendency to be cranky and irritable. As we cry out to God in these situations, I believe He'll answer us and give us the grace we need to respond in a way that will glorify Him.

Day Twenty-One

When I was very young, my parents rented a lake cabin in Alabama. We would go to the cabin quite often on summer weekends. The cabin had a screen door that opened to a few wooden steps, which led to the pathway down to the lake. One day we were walking down those steps and saw a snake underneath them. Of course we all freaked out and started running away from the snake (who was probably more scared than all of us). Daddy was a bit behind us and as he came down the steps we all started screaming and pointing, "A snake, a snake!"

Daddy stopped about mid-stair and started back up the steps thinking he was getting away from the snake. However, the snake had started climbing the concrete wall underneath the steps and was headed right for my Daddy's foot. Of course, we freaked out and yelled even more frantically and Daddy couldn't figure out what in the world he was supposed to do. Eventually he understood and ran down the steps. He tripped on the welcome mat and somersaulted into the yard, avoiding the terrifying (and terrified) little water snake.

Daddy was too close to the situation to realize what was happening.
His perspective was different from ours.
We could tell which direction he needed to go, but he was too close to the snake to figure it out. His confusion came from being too close to the situation.

Many times in our Christian lives we are too close to the situation to see clearly which direction to go. We have a lack of perspective so our tendency is to think, "There is no hope."

The next lie we'll look at together has many derivatives: ***"There is no hope...it's no use...nothing's ever going to change about this situation."***

The first verse I think of to counter this lie is Philippians 1:6 which says, "being confident of this, that he who began a good work in you will carry it on to completion until the day of Christ Jesus."

There is always hope with Jesus, my friends. Because He is the One who began this thing, and He promises to bring it to completion. The New American Standard translation of this verse says, He will "perfect" us. You are on a journey, sister! It began on the day you were conceived and it will be perfected on the day of Christ Jesus.

There was a group back in the 70s who sang a song with these lyrics:

Keep on walking
You don't know how far you've come
Keep on walking
For all you know it might be done
And the Father
Might be standing up right now
To give the call and end it all
So keep on walking.

Don't lose sight of the fact that this is a journey. We haven't arrived yet; we've still got a ways to go. It's okay to be imperfect. It's okay to not have everything figured out. You should not expect to be in complete control in every area of your life.

God doesn't want you to be perfect—He's the perfect One. He doesn't need for you to figure everything out--He's got it figured out. And He doesn't want you in control—He wants you dependent on the fact that He is in control.

Is there an area in your life in which you think there is no hope? Is there a place where you want change, but just can't see it happening? If you feel comfortable putting it on paper, write it here: (If not...just whisper it to Jesus. He already knows your heart.)

_____

_____

_____

I once heard a Bible teacher talking about looking at a panoramic view of who God is. I think her point was that as we look at what God has done for us over the course of our lifetime we will begin to get a better understanding of who He is and what His character is like.

Morning by morning
I wake up to find
The power and comfort of God's hand in mine
Season by season I watch Him amazed
In awe of the mystery of His
perfect ways
All I have need of His hand
will provide
He's always been faithful to me. ~ Sara Groves

I can look back over the seasons of my life and see many, many times when the Lord was faithful to me. There have been times of great joy and prosperity when I recognized His hand of blessing on my life. There have been some times of agonizing struggle when I realized that He was in the middle of it all, and He was using those trials to draw me to Himself. And there have also been times where I've felt like nothing was happening—no growth, no change, nothing. And yet, even in those times, God has been faithful.

It is His grace that calls me to cling to Him. He is the One who woos me to get up in the morning and think about Him. He is the One who draws me to Himself. I would be deceiving myself if I thought I was the one initiating this relationship. It's all Him. I can sing right along with Sara, "He's always been faithful to me."

Take a few minutes and look back over your life. Ask God to show you a panoramic view of His involvement with you. Make a note here of three different seasons when He has shown His faithfulness to you.

_____

_____

_____

_____

It's very easy to remember hard times. It's easy to dwell on trials and struggles. That's what the writer of Lamentations was doing in chapter three—remembering how hard it was to see Jerusalem destroyed and be carried into exile. But watch how he turns the corner in verse 21. Read Lamentations 3:1-29. This is not a particularly fun passage to read. This guy's pretty bummed out, probably like you may have been once or twice in your life. But look what happens in verse 21! He **chooses** to call something to mind. He makes a choice to remember something.

He writes, "Yet this I call to mind and therefore I have _____."

What does he call to mind?

Summarize verses 22 and 23 in your own words:

_____

_____

_____

I love that! I can almost see him stopping on purpose in the middle of his (very understandable) pity party to say,

"Oh yeah, but let me remind myself that
God is good."

And because he reminded himself of God's faithfulness he says,

"Therefore I have great HOPE!"

I'll say it once again, there is always hope with Jesus, my friends. Sometimes change doesn't happen as quickly as we would like or even in the same manner we would choose, but there is always hope. Our God is a God of hope.

Read verses 24- 26 and fill in the blanks:

I say to myself, "The LORD is my _____;
therefore I will wait for him."

What do you think the word 'portion' means here?

_____

_____

_____

Other versions translate this,

"The Lord is my 'share' or my 'inheritance'."
The Message says:

"He's all I've got left."
The LORD is good to those whose _____ is in him,
to the one who _____ him; it is good to _____ quietly
for the salvation of the LORD.

Let's finish up today by reading this passage in the Message. Let this translation wash over you and fill you with encouragement today.

Lamentations 3:9-30

I'll never forget the trouble, the utter lostness, the taste of ashes, the poison I've swallowed. I remember it all—oh, how well I remember— the feeling of hitting the bottom. But there's one other thing I remember, and remembering, I keep a grip on hope: God's loyal love couldn't have run out, his merciful love couldn't have dried up. They're created new every morning. How great your faithfulness!

I'm sticking with God (I say it over and over).
He's all I've got left. God proves to be good to the man who passionately waits, to the woman who diligently seeks. It's a good thing to quietly hope, quietly hope for help from God.

It's a good thing when you're young to stick it out through the hard times.
When life is heavy and hard to take, go off by yourself. Enter the silence.
Bow in prayer. Don't ask questions:
Wait for hope to appear.
Don't run from trouble. Take it full-face
The "worst" is never the worst.

Day Twenty-Two

On Day 16 we talked about negative self-talk and what to do with it. We decided that the right thing to do is to replace our negative thoughts with God's word! Yesterday we looked at a verse in Lamentations about the consistent faithfulness of God. And right there in the middle of the passage was an example of self-talk! Let's take a peek at this verse again. Look at Lamentations 3:24. Write the first four words:

____   _____   ____   _____

There it is...that's a huge key in this battle we're fighting in our minds: **What we say to ourselves.**

Do you ever get bummed out? I'm talking about for seemingly no good reason. You know, you wake up one morning and things just seem really dark. There's not a job crisis, no health issues, your circumstances seem to be okay, but your feelings are bleak. What's a woman to do?

When I'm feeling this way I like to go to Psalms 42 and 43. I believe in these two chapters we can find a very specific answer to this dilemma.

Psalm 42 opens with a passionate longing for God. The Psalmist compares his desire for God to the need for a deer to have water. He writes,

"My soul thirsts for God, for the living God. When can I go and meet with God?"

After this passionate plea, the Psalmist begins to lament about how he's been feeling, about tears and questions. He remembers how it used to be when things were good. And then he turns an interesting corner. Instead of talking or writing to others, the Psalmist begins in verse 5 to speak to himself. Self-talk! Right there in the Bible!

Psalm 42:5 says,

Why are you downcast, O my soul?
Why so disturbed within me?
Put your hope in God,
for I will yet praise him,
my Savior and my God.

The Message says,

Why are you down in the dumps, dear soul?
Why are you crying the blues? Fix my eyes on God—soon I'll be praising again.
He puts a smile on my face. He's my God.

The Psalmist is speaking to himself and saying, *"Hey, wait a minute, just what's going on here….Why am I so bummed out? This is God we're talking about! Surely when I think about how awesome He is I'll be encouraged again!"*

Rewrite this passage in your own words:

_____

_____

_____

Looking onto the next verse, he writes,

"My soul is downcast within me; therefore I will remember you…"

He recognizes that the solution for his discouragement is remembering the Lord! I will remember You! What a great thing for us to tell ourselves: **Remember the Lord.**

Remember, Jeanne (insert your name here), you have a God! He is not only a righteous judge, He is your Father! He will take care of you. He will take care of this situation you're freaking out about. He holds you in His righteous right hand! Remember all the good things He's done for you in the past. Remember what His word says about the future. Don't forget! You belong to God.

Brings comfort, doesn't it?

The next few verses of this Psalm seem to indicate that the Psalmist is vacillating wildly in his emotions. One minute he's overwhelmed, the next he's recognizing God's goodness, the next he's feeling rejected by God. Anybody ever had those kinds of irrational mood swings? It's amazing how quickly and easily this can happen.

Now here's where I think things get really interesting. The next verse goes like this: Verse 11 says,

> Why are you downcast,
> O my soul? Why so disturbed within me?
> Put your hope in God,
> for I will yet praise him,
> my Savior and my God.

Have you heard that anywhere before? Does it sound familiar? Maybe because it is a word for word repetition of verse 5! This "speaking to your soul" thing is something the Psalmist wanted to make sure we'd get. In fact, if you read on through Psalm 43, you'll find that the Psalm also closes with these exact words. It's as if these words serve as the chorus for these two chapters. They are repeated for emphasis. I think God wants us to see something here.

When we get discouraged, one of the ways out is to **encourage ourselves.** Yes, God gives us community, and He wants us to encourage each other. Yes, God will encourage us through His presence and by His Word, but I believe He also wants us to become proficient at encouraging ourselves. Speak to your soul! Talk yourself out of that discouragement! Do it with passion and on purpose!

It's not as if whoever wrote this Psalm was working on a computer with Microsoft Word installed. He didn't have the technology to right click, drag, copy and paste. These verses were repeated on purpose and for a purpose.

I noticed this same thing in Psalm 8. Let's look at that. What does the first verse of Psalm 8 proclaim?

_____

_____

_____

What is the middle of the chapter about?

_____
_____
_____
_____

And how does the Psalm end?

_____
_____
_____

"What is man?" is sandwiched between triumphant choruses of

"Oh Lord, our Lord, how majestic is Your name in all the earth!"

When something is written two or three times, it is on purpose and for emphasis, something we need to really grasp. Let's make sure that we do.

Don't let your eyes skim over scripture, my friends…not even the familiar passages. God wants to speak to you every single time you open His Word. The Holy Spirit is the One who leads us, even in small seemingly insignificant activities. If you are reading a verse of scripture, you can be assured that it is the Holy Spirit who has caused that to happen. Read it with a heart that longs to hear and respond.

Day Twenty-Three

We know of David, the shepherd boy who played a harp and sang songs to the Lord, We know of David as a young but brave giant killer and as a famous military genius who led his 'mighty men' in great military conquests. We know David as the popular and benevolent king of Israel. We also are familiar with David's well-known fall into sin with Bathsheba.

There is a lesser known account of David's life reported in 1 Samuel 29 in which he suffers a rejection. He had been living with his family, not in Israel, but actually in the country of Philistia. You remember, I'm sure, that the Philistines were enemies of Israel. During this season, David had been running away from King Saul because Saul was jealous of David's great military successes. Saul was trying to kill David and so the younger man was literally running for his life. He had been hiding in caves in Israel and finally left and settled in the land of their enemy, the Philistines. He and his men were soldiers, fighting in a faction of the Philistine army for a while. When the Philistines brought their military units together into one army to fight against Israel, David agreed to fight with them. The Philistine king, however, rejected David's service. He was afraid that David and his men would change their minds in the heat of the battle and reverse their loyalties. He worried that in the middle of a fight they might remember their homeland and switch sides!

It's hard to know how David might have felt after this rejection. You have to wonder if he really wanted to fight against Israel or if he was hoping to be denied. At any rate and for whatever reason, he was told him to go home...and when he got home, devastation awaited him.

Read 1 Samuel 30:1-6. This is the historical account of when David and his men returned from their mission to find that their homes in Ziklag had been destroyed by a different enemy and their wives and families had been taken captive.

He had every reason to be depressed, don't you think?

What does verse 4 say about their weeping?

_____

_____

And then things go from bad to worse as David realizes that his men are turning against him.

What did they discuss doing?

_____

_____

Yes, David was certainly feeling intense anxiety here.

How does scripture record that David responded?

_____

_____

Wow…David encouraged himself in the Lord. He found strength in the Lord. **David leaned into his relationship with God.** And what he found there was strength. David, the warrior, was the same man as David, the Psalmist. In times of great sorrow and fear, I believe David wrote his most powerful Psalms.

After David found strength in the Lord he allowed that strength to move him to action. Before acting, however, David took the time for an important step.

7 Then David said to Abiathar the priest, the son of Ahimelek, "Bring me the ephod." Abiathar brought it to him, 8 and David inquired of the Lord, "Shall I pursue this raiding party? Will I overtake them?"

According to verse 8, what did David do, before taking action?

_____

Oh, friends! That's such an important step! We have to remember to inquire of the Lord. We must take the time to ask and then to listen for the answer. It's so easy to get excited about something and to take off thinking that we know the best way, the right answer, the most influential pathway to take. But we don't. He does. Let's ask. And then wait. And listen. And then ask for the grace to obey.

David inquired of the Lord. God told him to go and there would be victory. So he did and there was…but it wasn't easy.

According to v.17, how long did the battle last?

_____

How much was David able to recover?

_____

Copy verses 18 and 19 here:

_____

_____

_____

_____

I love that David and his men were able to recover everything. The Lord completely protected their families for them. I love that.

I'd like to make two more points in our lesson today. Some of the men had been too exhausted to go into battle with the others and had stayed behind to rest. When the returning conquerors came with the plunder, some of them didn't want to share what had been recovered. But David generously proclaimed that all of the men in his forces would receive plunder. He said, "The share of the man who stayed with the supplies is to be the same as that of him who went down to the battle. All will share alike." 1 Samuel 30:24

David also sent some of the plunder to the elders of Judah who were his friends. My point here is simply that David was a generous man who recognized that his victory came from the Lord and not from his own hand. He was quick to share credit with others and was not arrogant or prideful. I want to be like that. Scripture calls David a man after God's own heart. I want to be like that, as well. A woman with a heart like Jesus.

In her book *Fresh-Brewed Life*, Nicole Johnson writes,
Allowing myself to listen to my longings rather than running from them, has radically changed me. Finding the courage to stare into the caverns of my own soul has fostered a dependency on God that I have not known before. Therein lies the treasure we seek. Longings are the map that will point the way…a fresh-brewed life will never mean the absence of pain. What it means is the presence of life. There is

no life without pain. No treasure without the hunt…Let's wake up and investigate the caverns.

Look up Psalm 139:23 and 24 and copy it here:

_____

_____

_____

_____

I believe there are times when God wants us to be introspective. He wants us to allow His Holy Spirit to shine His searchlight into our lives and reveal our true selves— our longings. It is in this kind of honest emotion that we draw the closest to Him. Nicole Johnson writes:

Each longing in my life that I have discovered, or that has discovered me, drives me to confront a truth that I might not have confronted otherwise: I need God. I am thirsty for God. Desperately thirsty. In every area of my life. I was made by Him and for Him, and apart from Him, I will not be satisfied.

Oh, friends, I agree with Nicole! There is a longing and a craving inside of me to know Jesus more fully! I want to be more like Him! I want to understand His will for my life and follow Him more completely today than I did yesterday. I'm sure that is your desire, too.

My prayer this morning is for the ability to lean into Jesus. Whether I'm rejoicing over victory, or agonizing over (temporary) defeat. Whatever the situation, I want my response to be to draw near to the ever-living, ever-loving God of the Universe. My longing is fulfilled only in Him.

Lord, Jesus, this morning I'm thinking about

_____

_____.

I am concerned that

_____

_____

_____.

Please help me to see Your involvement in this situation…Please help me to lean into my relationship with You today. I rejoice in who You are and what You are doing in my life. I choose to trust that You know what You are doing, and that You are completing a good work in me.

Thank you so much for Your goodness toward me. Let me hear Your voice today, whispering in my ear as I walk. I surrender _____
to You, knowing that You are in complete control and my circumstances are no surprise to You. Win or lose, O God...I choose to trust You with my life. Please help me to fully experience all You have for me this day. Amen.

Day Twenty-Four

I was driving to work but my mind wasn't on the road. I was completely immersed in the conversation I was having with my brother. We had been talking for some time and I was filling him in on what was going on in my life. The school where I worked was closing and many families were affected. Teachers were losing their jobs. Children would need to transfer to a different school. Not only were people disappointed and angry, but families' lives were changing drastically. Life was being shaken for a lot of different people. What was happening didn't seem to be at all right or fair and, worst of all, it was completely out of my control.

I tried to conclude the conversation by saying, "I'm just going through a really bad time." Glenn hesitated, took a deep breath, and said these words: "Jeanne, this is not a bad time, this is a hard time. And hard times are not bad times."

Wow. Now that was an innovative thought. You mean "hard" doesn't equate with "bad"? That doesn't sound like a red, white, and blue American thought to me! Aren't we supposed to be rich and strong and happy and blessed? Aren't we God's favorites? Isn't life supposed to be one big chorus of 'And They Lived Happily Ever After'? (insert sarcastic emoji here)

It's so easy to think that way. But that's not what the Bible teaches. And that's not the way it was for our Bible "heroes".

Yesterday our study took us to a time in David's life when he and his men wept until they had no more tears left to weep. Times are definitely hard when you have no more energy left to cry. There were plenty of hard times for the people who lived back in Bible times.

Joseph was a young man when his brothers sold him to Midianite merchants who were on their way to Egypt. He went quickly from being the favorite son of a rich man to a slave in a foreign country. Definitely hard times for Joe. But scripture tells us that even in this hard situation, Joseph found favor.

Look up Genesis 39: 2-4. What does this passage say about Joseph?

_____

_____

_____

_____

Daniel was certainly in a hard situation the night he spent in a den of hungry lions. Yet because of his deep relationship with the Lord, Daniel was saved. Write his response to King Darius here. You'll find it in Daniel 6:21.

_____

_____

_____

_____

Esther was raised up from being an orphan in exile to being the Queen of Persia. I'm sure her childhood years were difficult, yet the Lord used her in adulthood to rescue the entire nation of Jewish people.

Gideon lived through very difficult circumstances when the people of Israel were being oppressed by the Midianites. The angel of the Lord appeared to him and challenged him to deliver his people. Gideon was afraid and complained to the angel. He said, "How can I save Israel? My clan is the weakest and I am the least!" The Lord responded to Gideon with a reassuring promise. Look up Judges 6:16 and write God's promise to Gideon here:

_____

_____

_____

The book of Ruth tells the story of a young widow who immigrated to Judah and, as a foreigner, eventually found favor with the people there. The Lord blessed her because of her love toward her mother-in-law.

As we've discovered in our scripture study today, there was nothing
easy about these Bible character's lives. Each of them lived through some very hard days. Days where they could have whined and complained and talked on the phone a lot.

Actually, they may have done some complaining, because they were human. . .

but they persisted through the hard times. They kept on walking. They endured. Even though it was hard. They stayed connected to their God and allowed themselves to be used by Him. And they turned out becoming Bible heroes.

I don't know what's happening in your life right now. Could be any number of things. "Life is hard" can manifest itself in many ways. Health issues. Lack of employment. Relationships. Maybe you have teenagers! Or toddlers! Or both! (I'll pray for you.)

What are some of your concerns today?

_____

_____

_____

I read a story by Phillip Gulley about a guy who planted a yard full of oak trees but never watered them. He said if you watered them, it made them "sissy trees" and they'd never be strong. That if their roots were forced to go in search of water, that would make stronger trees in the long run.

Gulley is a fabulous storyteller and he concludes the tale by telling how he likes to pray over his sons after they've fallen asleep at night. His prayers have changed from "Lord, spare them from hardship," instead to a prayer that their roots would grow deep and draw strength from the eternal God.

I agree with that kind of prayer. Because life is hard. And we must stay connected to our eternal God. We draw our very life from Him. The same God who walked with those Bible characters walks with you and me today. Our roots can go down deep into the bedrock truth of that eternal God and find strength and nourishment there.

Hard times are not bad times, friend. They're when our roots go down deep into the eternal God.

Write a prayer of trust to the Lord today. Leave your concerns in His oh-so-capable hands.

_____

_____

_____

_____

_____

_____

Day Twenty-Five

John and I were driving through the Canadian Rockies. The roads were winding through the pointy pine trees; the mountains were bigger and more majestic than any I'd ever seen. The scenery was absolutely breath taking. We were filled with wonder and awe at the beauty of it all…and I was reading. A book. In the car, in the front seat, I was reading a book.

It was a book of lists that I'd gotten at Walmart before we left to go on our trip. I'd bought it because it looked interesting; it looked like something that would spark meaningful conversation between us. And it did…I would read a section or two aloud to John, and it would open the door for significant interaction and discussion…sometimes.

But this one time he got a little frustrated with me and said, "I can't believe you're reading a book! I bring you all the way up here to Canada to see these amazing sights, and you're reading a book!" I put the book away then, but I didn't stop thinking about the dialogue we'd just had. Why indeed, had I wanted to read instead of enjoy the beauty of the landscape?

It wasn't that I wasn't enjoying the mountains; I was loving the experience. I just wanted to add to it. Along with seeing the majestic scenery, I also wanted meaningful conversation with my husband. I was *longing for intimacy*. I was longing to discuss things that mattered. This book had chapters entitled: 'Life,' 'Marriage and Romance,' 'Contentment,' 'Teens,' 'Family Lessons,' and 'Wisdom.' I knew that as I read out loud it would trigger thoughts and discussion that we might not otherwise have. So I was reading, out loud, as I was looking and exclaiming over the magnificence outside my window.

I wanted both.

We long for intimacy. We long for deep and meaningful conversations. There is something inside of every human being that wants to be touched in a significant way. I wanted to do more than look. I wanted to feel.

I want that in my relationship with God, too. Yes, I absolutely want the wonder and awe of His amazing Word. I want to read and study and memorize and apply His Word. It is my source of direction and complete truth. It has answers to every situation; it is full of understanding and wisdom.

But I want more. I want intimacy. I want meaningful conversation with my Father God and with Jesus, the lover of my soul. I want to know Him. I long to be known by Him. I long for that. I yearn for that. My soul craves that more than anything.

Look up Psalm 63:1. How does the Psalmist describe his intense desire for God?

_____

_____

_____

How does the Psalmist describe his current surroundings?

_____

_____

_____

Read Isaiah 58:11. What does this scripture say the Lord will do 'in a sun-scorched land?

_____

_____

One of our deepest needs is to be known. God says He is the One who will satisfy that need.

Copy Isaiah 58:11 here. Let the words of this verse sink down into your thirsty soul.

_____

_____

_____

_____

_____

_____

Look up Psalm 42: 1 and 2 and fill in the blanks:

As the deer _____ for streams of water,

So my soul _____ for you, O God.

My soul _____ for God, for the living God. When can I go and meet with God?

Now here's a really cool thing about God. The Psalmist asks the rhetorical question, "When can I go and meet with God?" And the answer is this: NOW! Right now! Any time! He is there. He is available. He is waiting; longing really, for us to come and meet with Him. James 4:8 tells us that if we draw near to the Lord, He will draw near to us.

Look up Isaiah 65:24. When does the Lord say He will answer?

_____

_ Scripture tells us that the Lord longs to be gracious to us.

Yet the Lord longs to be gracious to you; therefore he will rise up to show you

compassion. Isaiah 30:18

Intimacy is what the Psalmist is looking for in Psalm 42—an intimate and fulfilling relationship with the Lord. He knows that God is the only One who can fill up the empty places. He recognizes his needs will only be met by the Living God.

Psalm 73:28 says that it is good for us to draw near to God. This verse says "I have made the Sovereign Lord my_____."

Look back at the end of Isaiah 58:11. What does that verse say that God will make you into? As a result of allowing Him to satisfy your needs, God promises to make you into:

_____

_____

_____

Look up John 7:37-39 for a corresponding New Testament passage. Jesus said, "If any man _____, let him come to Me..."

Then He promises that out of believers will flow _____ of living water.

How interesting…God made us to long for intimacy. He created us to crave Him.

God promises that He will fill up the longing in our hearts. And in filling it up, he will cause us to be satisfying to others. My prayer for you today, my friend, is that you will be so tight with Jesus that you are filled and flooded with His love and His joy and His contentment. And may that love and joy and contentment splash out onto the people around today in a way that makes them thirsty for a relationship with Him.

Day Twenty-Six

How many of you have had a toddler cry when you flushed the toilet for him? "I can do it myself!" he exclaims, distraught that you had the audacity to flush HIS poop! How many times have you given that same toddler his own spoon to try to scoop up his peas and navigate them toward his precious little mouth without losing every single pea in the process? His longing is for independence! "I'm a big kid now, I don't need diapers, I don't need a lid on my cup, I don't want you to do it, I can do it myself!"

This is a very natural stage of development. The child God gave to you is beginning to work his way toward adulthood…as it was intended to be.

Let's take this out of the context of parent/child relationships and look at what this might mean to us as mature Christians. Is it okay to be independent? "Is it right to say, I can do it myself; I don't need anyone else"? Or, is it possible that this is a lie we need to recognize and replace with the truth of God's word? Where's the balance? What's the truth?

When we proclaim, "I can do it myself," to our Christian brothers and sisters, I wonder if what we're actually saying is this: "I don't really need you. Me and Jesus-- we've got our own thing going. Jesus is all I need to make it through this life."

The problem with this faulty thinking is that Jesus is the One who created community in the first place. He created us to need each other. Actually, before He created anything, there was community. In the Trinity of Father, Son and Holy Spirit, relationship was birthed. They needed each other. If we are created in their image, how can we be any different? Even as God created the family to bring children to maturity, He made the church to bring Christians to a place of maturity. The community of the church, the body of Christ, is required for one to grow to spiritual maturity.

Let's take a look at a guy named Saul. When we're first introduced to Saul, he appears to be very independent.

Read:
Acts 7:57-59
Acts 8:1-3
Acts 9:1-2
What was Saul doing the first time he's mentioned in scripture?

_____

_____

What was the purpose of Saul's trip?

_____

_____

Now read:
Acts 9:3-31

After this amazing conversion experience, Saul spent several days with the believers who lived in Damascus. While there, he met a guy named Barnabas, who would become one of his closest friends. Barnabas's name had been changed from 'Joseph' to 'Barnabas', which means 'son of encouragement'. Barnabas took Saul back to Jerusalem and introduced him to the apostles and believers there.

Beth Moore writes of Barnabas:
God used Barnabas over and over to give others the courage to be the people he called them to be. When Barnabas brought Saul before the other apostles, they may have remembered how each of them had been the focus of his encouragement at one time or another. Now he encouraged them to accept a new brother...Barnabas persuaded the apostles to accept the new convert, and the most powerful preacher in all Christendom was set loose in Jerusalem.

Saul, also known as Paul, learned through Barnabas how to build and rely on godly friendships. For six years they ministered together. When God led them in different directions, it is clear that Paul built similar relationships with others who would travel with him. In the epistles that Paul writes, he mentions over and over again, people he wants to greet. These personal messages are written to people he has enjoyed relationships with throughout his time of ministry in the early church.

Read Colossians 4:7-18
How many different people does Paul mention by name?

_____

_____

I'm telling you, Paul lived in community, and he deeply loved the people with whom he lived and worked. He also deeply loved those he to whom he was writing.
Read Philippians 1:3-8
How does Paul describe his deep love for these people?

Verse 7 says, "It is right for me to feel this way about all of you, since _____ _____

____ ___ ___ _____." Verse 8 continues "God can testify how I _____ ___

_____ __ _____ with the _____ of Christ Jesus."

The point I'm making, my friends, is that this man who began his adulthood by "uttering murderous threats" against believers in the Way, became a man who loved and longed for community. He was no longer independent. He recognized his dependence on the body of Christ. In the final letter Paul wrote, he greets Timothy, his spiritual son with the words, "Recalling your tears, I long to see you so that I may be filled with joy."

Here is a man who loved with his whole heart. He knew he couldn't "do it by himself"… and he didn't want to.

Finish your Bible study time this morning by thanking the Lord for the people He has placed in your community. This may include family as well as friends and church members. Give the Lord praise for the people He has place in your life. Ask Him to make you a blessing to each of them as well!

Day Twenty-Seven

"In isolation we die; in interdependence we live."—Madeline L'Engle

I remember leaving my Kearney Bible Study one Tuesday. I was carrying my guitar and a heavy amplifier. As I came to two sets of double glass doors, I had to struggle and lean against the doors with my well-padded bottom, but I was able to make it out by myself. As I walked through, my friend Debbie hurried up behind me, wanting to help. I made it through before she got there. She shook her head and said, "You are so independent!" The thing that puzzled me a bit was that she said it like it was something bad!

I like it that I can do things myself. My father-in-law called me a 'can-do girl.' I liked that! But here's the deal…maybe Debbie was put in my life to help me. (Undoubtedly she was… in so many ways other than holding a door). When we insist on doing everything by ourselves, we miss out on a very important aspect of life: community.

Yesterday we saw how the Christian-hating Pharisee, Saul, became the amazing lover of the first Christians and writer of much of the New Testament, Paul. He grew from being independent and self-righteous, to being interdependent with many members of the early Church.

Today I'd like to continue looking at scriptures that will bring truth to the faulty thinking of "I can do it by myself." Scripture makes it very clear that we need each other.

Look up Galatians 6:2. What does this scripture encourage us to do with each other's burdens?

_____

_____

Depending on the version you read, your answer may be bear one another's burdens (NASV), carry each other's burdens (NIV), or share each other's burdens (NLT).

The Contemporary English Version translates this: *"You obey the law of Christ when you offer each other a helping hand."* (I should have let Debbie help me with the door. That's the Biblical thing to do.)

The Message reads, *"Stoop down and reach out to those who are oppressed. Share their burdens, and so complete Christ's law."*

Regardless of the translation you read, it is clear that we are to be involved in each other's lives. God calls no one to be a 'lone ranger.' The wisest man in history writes about relationship in Ecclesiastes 4:9-12. Read this passage and answer the following:

Why are two better than one?

_____

_____

(I was teaching this to second graders several years ago. When I asked them what the word 'labor' means, one little guy whose mother was a midwife started, "Well, it's like when a woman is having a baby and...")

What happens if one falls down?

_____

_____

When two lie down together, what's the benefit?

_____

_____

And finally, what does this scripture say is 'not easily broken'?

_____

_____

Who do you reckon is the 'third strand' here?

_____

(of course, it is!)

Look up Proverbs 27:17 and copy it here:

_____
_____

The New Living Translation says, "As iron sharpens iron, so a friend sharpens a friend." Proverbs 27:17

I'm telling you, ladies, friendships with other believers in Christ are crucial to our success as Christian women. If we are going to stay sharp in our believing lies and rejecting truth, we need each other's help. We need to hold each other accountable in this battle against falsehood. If you don't have close Christian girlfriends, *please* reach out *today* and connect with another woman in your church body! Chances are, that woman is just as lonely as you are, and she's waiting to hear from a friend.

In his book, <u>The Naked Life</u>, Duncan Banks writes,

I can think of certain people in my world whose company invigorates me, and when they leave I am full of resolve, ideas and intentions about God, self-improvement and service to others...we must also cultivate significant time in friendship with people who will spark energy in us.

Just last week someone said to me, "You have a huge capacity for relationship." That's true. I do! I love people, especially the ones I can call 'friend,' and God has given me many.

There's a group of women I meet with once a week on Tuesday nights. We call ourselves an 'accountability group,' and I guess that's what we are, but it feels to me like what we do is get together and visit. We talk about all kinds of things, and eventually share concerns and promise to pray for each other. This is a fun group! Tuesday nights are one of my favorite parts of my week. It's not a drag to invest yourself in others, it's a pleasure and an honor.

My 'Debbies' are friends I've known longer. I met Debbie, Debbie, Lee Ann, and Ronda when our children were in elementary school, and now our children are grown with children of their own. These women have loved me, counseled me, confronted me, and encouraged me for many years. Meeting with them regularly is a priority in my life.

And then there are my TLF buds. These gals go all the way back to college days. There are only three of us in this group: one from Spokane, WA, one from Portland, OR, and myself from right here in Kearney, MO. We get together either here in the

Mid-West, or somewhere in the Pacific Northwest, at least every other year. We like to meet annually, but that doesn't always happen. With these two, although we live on opposite ends of the world, when we get together after a long separation, it's as if nothing has changed. These are friends of my life.

These three groups of women provide a foundation for me. I feel more secure in decisions I make if I've had a chance to talk things over with these buddies. There is wisdom in counsel, and these girls are my counselors (for the price of a cup of coffee as opposed to paying for an hour of therapy!). Having these kinds of relationships provides a structure for my life that is hugely beneficial to me.

I am also extremely blessed to have rewarding relationships within my own family. My siblings and parents play very instrumental roles in my life. Of course, my husband is my best counselor and biggest support of all. Interestingly, as they've grown, my children have also become sources of good insight and counsel on occasion. I am very blessed in the realm of relationship.

I truly believe that God created us to need each other and there is great benefit to this. As we become more interdependent our intimacy increases. Our husbands want to be needed. Our friends want to be needed. God wants us to recognize how much we need Him. Independence is not the goal—interdependence is.

In her book <u>Every Thought Captive</u>, Jerusha Clark explains the importance of relationships:

I love the way Lauren Winner describes friendship in her memoir <u>Girl Meets God</u>. She writes, 'There are a few people out there with whom you fit just so, and amazingly, you keep fitting just so even after you have growth spurts or lose weight or stop wearing high heels. You keep fitting after you have children…or stop dyeing your hair or quit your job…and take up farming. Somehow, God is gracious enough to give us a few of those people, people you can stretch into, people who don't go away, and whom you wouldn't want to go away, even if they offered to.'

*We need to find these people because **they will help us live out truth** over the long haul. We need to find these people because they will be able to see when we've fallen into old thought patterns, often before we see it ourselves. And we need to find these people because they are lovely, fun, and a source of amazing sustenance.*

Make a list of those you can call "friend". Write a few notes, shoot off a text or an email…Let these friends know you're thinking about them today.

111

Day Twenty-Eight
Metamorphosis of the Mind:
Experiencing Jesus as the Truth

Day Twenty-Eight

When Phillip was a little guy he would occasionally get his words confused. The interesting thing was that his confusion almost always made sense in some way. For example, when he wanted to sit beside me, he would say "I wanna sit **by** next to you, Mama." (Instead of **right** next to you...He knew it had something to do with being by me...)

One day all of the cousins had gathered at Aunt Gayle's house. She had some work she needed to do without distractions, so I began to gather up all of the children to go to the park. Phillip said he didn't want to leave Aunt Gayle behind because he didn't want her to be **'only'**. In his little three year old mind, 'lonely' meant you were only by yourself and that was what was about to happen to Aunt Gayle...He didn't want her to feel **'only'**.

What Phillip didn't know is that feeling lonely isn't always the result of being alone. A person may feel lonely while in the middle of a crowd... a spouse may feel lonely even in marriage...a child may feel lonely even in the midst of family life.

One of Satan's schemes is to try to get us to believe that we are alone. A lie commonly believed by many women today is this: **"I'm all alone, no one really understands what I'm going through."** This is actually a lie on several different levels. Undoubtedly there are others somewhere in this universe who have lived under similar circumstances. Probably there are those quite close to us who are experiencing the same kind of situations. More importantly, however, and more assuredly, *we are not alone because of the presence and involvement of God in our lives.*

The birth of Jesus is foretold in Isaiah 7:14. Complete the following:
Therefore the Lord himself will give you a sign: The _____ will be with child and will give birth to a _____, and will call him_____.

This scripture is quoted in Matthew 1:23, along with a translation of the name Immanuel. Complete the following: *"The _____ will be with child and will give birth*

to a _____, and they will call him _____"—which means,
"_____ _____."

That's the whole reason Jesus came! To re-establish fellowship between mankind and God! He came **to be with us**…to live in us…to make His home with us.

Read Revelation 3:20 and complete:
_____ ___ _____! I stand at the door and knock. If anyone hears my voice and opens the door, ___ _____ _____ _____ and eat with him, and he with me.

Jesus Christ is the fulfillment of the One foretold in the Old Testament. He is Immanuel, God with us! He is God incarnate, the Word made flesh; He came to dwell among us. We are never alone.

Let's take a look at an Old Testament character who had every reason to believe he was alone. As a teenager, Joseph was betrayed and deserted by his own brothers and sold into slavery. He was taken far away from his home and country into a foreign culture where he knew no one. This boy had a reason to feel alone…

Read Genesis 39. After you've read the entire chapter, complete the following verses:

Vs. 2 The _____ _____ _____ _____ and he prospered, and he lived in the house of his Egyptian master.

Vs. 3 When his master saw that _____ _____ _____ _____ _____ and that the LORD gave him success in everything he did, Joseph found favor in his eyes and became his attendant.

Vs. 20-21 But while Joseph was there in the prison, _____ _____ _____ _____ _____; he showed him kindness and granted him favor in the eyes of the prison warden,

Vs. 23 The warden paid no attention to anything under Joseph's care, because _____ _____ _____ _____ _____ and gave him success in whatever he did.

Are you seeing a theme here? Even though Joseph was struggling with very unfair circumstances, scripture records over and over again that he was not alone. The Lord was with Joseph…as a slave…as a prisoner…and eventually as the ruler over Egypt.

Complete Genesis 41:38.
So Pharaoh asked them, "Can we find anyone like this man, _____ ____ _____ is the _____ of _____?"

The very Spirit of God lived inside of Joseph…the Lord was with him, through it all. I find great comfort in this…I believe that even as the Lord was with Joseph, He is with me. And He is with you. Regardless of where you find yourself. In prosperity…in poverty….in freedom…in slavery…no matter what, I believe we can have the assurance of the presence of the Lord.

*Colossians 1:27 To them, (the saints), God has chosen to make known among the Gentiles the glorious riches of this mystery, which is **Christ in you**, the hope of glory.*

This is indeed a mystery. It doesn't make sense to us, but it is truth, my friends…You are not alone. Christ lives in you and is your Source of great hope.

Not only is He a source of great hope, He promises to bear your burdens for you.

Let's take a look at some scriptures that promise God's presence to the believer.

Psalm 23:4
Even when I walk through the darkest valley, I will not be afraid, for you are _____
_____ _____Psalms 23:4 NLT

When you go through deep water ___ _____ ____ _____ ____ . Isaiah 43:2

And be sure of this: ____ ____ _____ ____ _____, even to the end of the age. Matthew 28:20 NLT

For God has said, "I will never fail you. I will never_____ _____"Hebrews 13:5 NLT

Are you struggling with unfair circumstances today? Do you feel like nobody understands where you're coming from? Are you just wishing you had someone who would walk alongside you? You do...His name is Jesus, Immanuel...God with us. He has re-established fellowship between you and God! He promises to carry your burdens for you! Let Him be the One. Choose to believe the truth today that God is with you, that Jesus lives in you, and that you are not alone.

Close your study today by writing out a prayer of trust in this One who walks along beside you. Commit your unfair circumstances to Him and allow Him to breathe hope into your life.

_____

_____

_____

_____

_____

_____

Day Twenty-Nine

All of my children's lives I've prayed that God would show them their 'kingdom task.' I believe that He has a job for each of us...many jobs, in fact. He has a purpose for placing us on this earth, in this country, in this state, in this town, in this church, in this family. God did not create you randomly. He has a reason and a purpose for your existence.

In light of this, what I'm saying when I mutter to myself *"I am insignificant"* is this: "I don't feel like I'm accomplishing anything for the Lord at this point in my life. What's going on? Why am I in this stagnant place?"

Many biblical characters experience 'wilderness' seasons.

David, the shepherd boy who had been anointed to be king, found himself unexpectedly in a wilderness season. At one point early in his life, David was running for his life from Saul, the current king of Israel. Beth Moore writes, "Filled with dreams and wonderful expectations, young David was met by a nightmare. He had not only left his home, now he ran from his 'home away from home.'

Read 1 Samuel 22:1. Where did David hide when he escaped from Gath?

_____

_____

At this point in his life, David was probably questioning his significance. He remembers that Samuel came and anointed him. He remembers the calling that is on his life, yet, here he is...hiding in a cave from a madman. He may be wondering how in the world he ended up in a situation like this. He quite possibly may be longing for the safety and satisfaction of tending sheep.

"Speak to me, speak to me in my cave of Adullam.
Reach to me, reach to me. No one cares for my
soul. I thought I saw your kingdom,
but it's not going to happen like I thought it would happen.

Remind me, remind me of the vision you gave me.
Remind me, remind me what anointing oil is for.
I need to know you're near me.
I need to know you are holding me just as closely,
As the day you took my life and gave me a vision,
As the day you poured the oil and gave me a dream.
I can't believe this is happening.
How does a shepherd become a king?" ~Sara Groves

It was in this very cave of Adullum that David wrote some of his Psalms.

Read Ps 57.

Write out a verse by verse progression of the emotions David may have been feeling as he wrote this.

Vs. 1 ~ *Have mercy on me! I'm safe in You!*

_____

Vs. 2 ~ *I cry out to God who fulfills His purpose for me.*

_____

Vs. 3 ~ *God sends His love and His faithfulness to me.*

_____

Vs. 4 ~ *I'm surrounded by men as fierce as animals!*

_____

Vs. 5 ~ *Be exalted, O God! Let Your glory cover the earth!*

_____

Vs. 6 ~ *They tried to trap me, but got trapped themselves.*

_____

Vs. 7 ~ *My heart is steadfast to the point that I can sing about it.*

_____

Vs. 8 ~ *Wake up, my soul! I will get up at dawn!*

_____

_ Vs. 9 ~ *Praise You, O Lord! I will sing about you to everybody!*

Vs. 10 ~ *Your love is as great as the heavens, your faithfulness as the sky.*

Vs. 11. ~ *Be exalted, O God! Let Your glory cover the earth!*

I'm encouraged that David not only confesses his fear, he also confesses what he knows to be true about God. He doesn't deny the fact that he's surrounded by fierce and dangerous men, but he places his focus on the fact that God is faithful and worthy to be praised.

I love the part of verse two where he proclaims it is God who fulfills His purpose for David's life. It's not David making sure some purpose is fulfilled, it's not a group of men who will make this kingdom come to pass, it is God who will do it.

Look up 1 Thessalonians 5:24.
Who is faithful?

Who will do it?

Sitting on a balcony looking out at the Gulf of Mexico, listening to the sounds of heavy machinery building a hotel next door, I felt the Lord say to me. "Quit trying to change the landscape, Jeanne...you're just making noise that interferes with the rhythms of my grace...It's not up to you to change yourself. It's not up to you to change the world. Relax. I am faithful. I am at work."

Do you feel like you're stagnating? Do you wonder what in the world is happening in your life? Are you finding yourself in some scary situations? I'm here to tell you that God is not surprised. He's not wondering what's going on. This is all part of His plan and His purpose.

He is faithful...He is the One who brings it to pass. Stop worrying, stop striving, relax and let Him be the One who changes the landscape of your life. Wilderness time is necessary for growth. Don't despise it. It's okay to be very honest with the

Lord and tell Him how you feel, but also remind yourself of his faithfulness. Trust the Lord, the lover of your soul. Whether you recognize it or not, He knows what He's doing. He really does.

Day Thirty

1 Kings 3:16-28(ESV)

Solomon's Wisdom

16 Then two prostitutes came to the king and stood before him. 17 The one woman said, "Oh, my lord, this woman and I live in the same house, and I gave birth to a child while she was in the house. 18 Then on the third day after I gave birth, this woman also gave birth. And we were alone. There was no one else with us in the house; only we two were in the house. 19 And this woman's son died in the night, because she lay on him. 20 And she arose at midnight and took my son from beside me, while your servant slept, and laid him at her breast, and laid her dead son at my breast. 21 When I rose in the morning to nurse my child, behold, he was dead. But when I looked at him closely in the morning, behold, he was not the child that I had borne." 22 But the other woman said, "No, the living child is mine, and the dead child is yours." The first said, "No, the dead child is yours, and the living child is mine." Thus they spoke before the king.

23 Then the king said, "The one says, 'This is my son that is alive, and your son is dead'; and the other says, 'No; but your son is dead, and my son is the living one.'" 24 And the king said, "Bring me a sword." So a sword was brought before the king. 25 And the king said, "Divide the living child in two, and give half to the one and half to the other." 26 Then the woman whose son was alive said to the king, because her heart yearned for her son, "Oh, my lord, give her the living child, and by no means put him to death." But the other said, "He shall be neither mine nor yours; divide him." 27 Then the king answered and said, "Give the living child to the first woman, and by no means put him to death; she is his mother." 28 And all

Israel heard of the judgment that the king had rendered, and they stood in awe of the king, because they perceived that the wisdom of God was in him to do justice.

Solomon was known throughout the world for his wisdom. When these women came to him to decide who the real mother was, Solomon didn't destroy the baby. He never intended to. He destroyed the scheme. He destroyed the lie. When he declared "Bring me a sword!" I can imagine the hearts of both mothers began to race. I imagine both women began to fear, perhaps, for their own lives, not only the life of the child. But Solomon wasn't really interested in killing anything... other than the deception. He was looking for truth. He knew this would reveal genuine maternal affection. The real mother was discovered when, in heartfelt compassion, she cried, "Don't kill the child! Give the baby to her! Please let my baby live!" That's wisdom.

Do you know how Solomon became so wise? It wasn't from going to school. He didn't get his masters in Wisdomology...nope. There was no PhD in the study of Wise Thinking. Scripture tells us how this came about in 1 Kings 3.

Solomon was King David's son and he became king after David's death.
Using 1 Kings 3: 5-15 as reference, what did God say to Solomon in a dream?

_____

_____

How did Solomon respond to God?

_____

_____

And what was God's reaction to Solomon's request?

_____

_____

Look up James1:5 and copy it here:

_____

_____

_____

_____

So, just like Solomon, we can ask the Lord for wisdom, and expect Him to give it to us. This is great news, because we need wisdom like crazy to be able to recognize the lies that permeate this culture we live in. This is wisdom:

- o Recognizing lies
- o Calling them what they are
- o Replacing them with the truth of God's word
- o Believing that truth

We can ask God to help us learn to do this! He's our heavenly Father, our Daddy. And He wants to teach us things, He wants to train us in righteousness. He wants us to grow and learn skills for living life, just like any father wants his child to grow and develop. So we can simply ask. We can pray, *"Please, Father, give me wisdom to recognize when the enemy, the father of lies is trying to trick me. Help me see his deception. Open my eyes to recognize his tricks. Let me hear You, Holy Spirit, whisper the truth of the Bible in my ear. Help me remember scriptures that I've studied that relate to this lie Satan is trying to get me to believe. Cause me to believe TRUTH, please, Lord. I want to believe the truth."*

In closing, let's look, once again at the two main verses this study has been centered around.

Copy Romans 12:2 from your favorite translation here:

_____

_____

_____

_____

_____

Copy 2 Corinthians 10:5 from your favorite translation here:

_____

_____

_____

_____

_____

Having completed this study, my hope is that you and I have indeed seen our minds changed; metamorphosed, by the transforming power of the Word of God. We can't help but be closer to the Lord. Thank you for joining me on this six week journey. I pray that our thoughts are more like Christ's, that our character has been conformed more into His image. My hope is that you have grown to love Bible study more. I also hope that you have enjoyed your time with these stories, thoughts and scriptures. I've surely enjoyed sharing them.

Scripture Index

DAY ONE

Revelation 20:3 He threw him into the Abyss, and locked and sealed it over him, to keep him from deceiving the nations anymore until the thousand years were ended. After that, he must be set free for a short time. (NIV)

7 When the thousand years are over, Satan will be released from his prison. (NIV)

10 And the devil, who deceived them, was thrown into the lake of burning sulfur, where the beast and the false prophet had been thrown. They will be tormented day and night for ever and ever.

Hosea 4:6 - My people are ruined because they don't know what's right or true. (MSG)

DAY TWO

Matthew 14:13 When Jesus heard what had happened, he withdrew by boat privately to a solitary place. Hearing of this, the crowds followed him on foot from the towns.

Matthew 14:23 After he had dismissed them, he went up on a mountainside by himself to pray. When evening came, he was there alone,

Mark 1:35 Very early in the morning, while it was still dark, Jesus got up, left the house and went off to a solitary place, where he prayed.

Luke 5:16 But Jesus often withdrew to lonely places and prayed.

DAY THREE

John 17:17 Sanctify them by the truth; your word is truth.

Jeremiah 29:13 (HCSB) 13 You will seek Me and find Me when you search for Me with all your heart.

DAY FOUR

Exodus 33:7-11 It was Moses' practice to take the Tent of Meeting and set it up some distance from the camp. Everyone who wanted to make a request of the LORD would go to the Tent of Meeting outside the
camp. Whenever Moses went out to the Tent of Meeting, all the people would get up and stand in the entrances of their own tents. They would all watch Moses until he disappeared inside. As he went into the tent, the pillar of cloud would come down and hover at its entrance while the LORD spoke with Moses. When the people saw the cloud standing at the entrance of the tent, they would stand and bow down in front of their own tents. Inside the Tent of Meeting, the LORD would speak to Moses face to face, as one speaks to a friend. Afterward Moses would return to the camp, but the young man who assisted him, Joshua son of Nun, would remain behind in the Tent of Meeting. (NLT)

DAY FIVE

James 4:8 Draw near to God and He will draw near to you

Psalm 73:28 But as for me, the nearness of God is my good; I have made the Lord GOD my refuge, that I may tell of all Your works.

DAY SIX

Isaiah 43:4 Since you are precious and honored in my sight, and because I love you, I will give men in exchange for you, and people in exchange for your life.

James 2:23 And the scripture was fulfilled that says, "Abraham believed God, and it was credited to him as righteousness," and he was called God's friend.

2 Chronicles 20:7 O our God, did you not drive out the inhabitants of this land before your people Israel and give it forever to the descendants of Abraham your friend?

Isaiah 41:8 But you, O Israel, my servant, Jacob, whom I have chosen, you descendants of Abraham my friend.

Luke 7:34 The Son of Man came eating and drinking, and you say, 'Here is a glutton and a drunkard, a friend of tax collectors and "sinners."

DAY SEVEN

1 Chronicles 15:23-24- Berekiah and Elkanah were to be doorkeepers for the ark. Shebaniah, Joshaphat, .Nethanel, Amasai, Zechariah, Benaiah and Eliezer the priests were to blow trumpets before the ark of God. Obed- Edom and Jehiah were also to be doorkeepers for the ark.

1 Chronicles 16: 4-6 He appointed some of the Levites to minister before the ark of the LORD, to make petition, to give thanks, and to praise the LORD, the God of Israel: Asaph was the chief, Zechariah second, then Jeiel, Shemiramoth, Jehiel, Mattithiah, Eliab, Benaiah, Obed-Edom and Jeiel. They were to play the lyres and harps; Asaph was to sound the cymbals,

and Jahaziel the priests were to blow the trumpets regularly before the ark of the covenant of God.

Psalm 91 –

1

He who dwells in the shelter of the Most High will rest in the shadow of the Almighty.

2

I will say of the LORD, "He is my refuge and my fortress, my God, in whom I trust."

3

Surely he will save you from the fowler's snare and from the deadly pestilence.

4

He will cover you with his feathers,
and under his wings you will find refuge;
his faithfulness will be your shield and rampart.

5

You will not fear the terror of night, nor the arrow that flies by day,

6

nor the pestilence that stalks in the darkness, nor the plague that destroys at midday.

7

A thousand may fall at your side, ten thousand at your right hand, but it will not come near you.

8

You will only observe with your eyes
and see the punishment of the wicked.

9

If you make the Most High your dwelling— even the LORD, who is my refuge-

10

then no harm will befall you,
no disaster will come near your tent.

11

For he will command his angels concerning you to guard you in all your ways;

12

    they will lift you up in their hands,
so that you will not strike your foot against a stone.

13

    You will tread upon the lion and the cobra;
you will trample the great lion and the serpent.

14

    "Because he loves me," says the LORD, "I will rescue him; I will protect him, for he acknowledges my name.

15

    He will call upon me, and I will answer him; I will be with him in trouble,
I will deliver him and honor him.

16

    With long life will I satisfy him and show him my salvation."

DAY EIGHT

Psalm 17:15 And I—in righteousness I will see your face; when I awake, I will be satisfied with seeing your likeness.

Isaiah 58:11 The LORD will guide you always; he will satisfy your needs in a sun-scorched land and will strengthen your frame. You will be like a well-watered garden, like a spring whose waters never fail.

Song of Solomon 2:14b Show me your face, let me hear your voice; for your voice is sweet, and your face is lovely.

DAY NINE

Psalm 119:105 Your word is a lamp to my feet and a light for my path.

John 10:10- The thief comes only to steal and kill and destroy; I have come that they may have life, and have it to the full.

DAY ELEVEN

Jeremiah 29:13-14 - You will seek me and find me when you seek me with all your heart. "When you come looking for me, you'll find me. "Yes, when you get serious about finding me and want it more than anything else, I'll make sure you won't be disappointed." GOD's Decree. "I'll turn things around for you. I'll bring you back from all the countries into which I drove you"—GOD's Decree—"bring you home to the place from which I sent you off into exile. You can count on it. (MSG)

DAY TWELVE

Romans 12:2 Do not conform any longer to the pattern of this world, but be transformed by the renewing of your mind. Then you will be able to test and approve what God's will is—his good, pleasing and perfect will.

Romans 12:2 So here's what I want you to do, God helping you: Take your everyday, ordinary life—your sleeping, eating, going-to-work, and walking-around life—and place it before God as an offering. Embracing what God does for you is the best thing you can do for him. Don't become so well-adjusted to your culture that you fit into it without even thinking. Instead, fix your attention on God. You'll be changed from the inside out. Readily recognize what he wants from you, and quickly respond to it. Unlike the culture around you, always dragging you down to its level of immaturity, God brings the best out of you, develops well-formed maturity in you. (MSG)

DAY THIRTEEN

Acts 22:3-16 Then Paul said: I am a Jew, born in Tarsus of Cilicia, but brought up in this city. Under Gamaliel I was thoroughly trained in the law of our fathers and was just as zealous for God as any of you are today. I persecuted the followers of this Way to their death, arresting both men and women and throwing them into prison, as also the high priest and all the Council can testify. I even obtained letters from them to their brothers in Damascus, and went there to bring these people as prisoners to Jerusalem to be punished. "About noon as I came near Damascus, suddenly a bright light from heaven flashed around me. I fell to the ground and heard a voice say to me, 'Saul! Saul! Why do you persecute me?' " 'Who are you, Lord?' I asked. " 'I am Jesus of Nazareth, whom you are persecuting,' he replied. My companions saw the light, but they did not understand the voice of him who was speaking to me.

"'What shall I do, Lord?' I asked.
"'Get up,' the Lord said, 'and go into Damascus. There you will be told all that you have been assigned to

do.' My companions led me by the hand into Damascus, because the brilliance of the light had blinded me.

"A man named Ananias came to see me. He was a devout observer of the law and highly respected by all the Jews living there. He stood beside me and said, 'Brother Saul, receive your sight!' And at that very moment I was able to see him.

"Then he said: 'The God of our fathers has chosen you to know his will and to see the Righteous One and to hear words from his mouth, you will be his witness to all men of what you have seen and heard. And now what are you waiting for? Get up, be baptized and wash your sins away, calling on his name.'

DAY FOURTEEN

John 14:16-17 And I will ask the Father, and he will give you another Counselor to be with you forever— the Spirit of truth. The world cannot accept him, because it neither sees him nor knows him. But you know him, for he lives with you and will be in you.

John 16:13 But when he, the Spirit of truth, comes, he will guide you into all truth. He will not speak on his own; he will speak only what he hears, and he will tell you what is yet to come.

2 Thessalonians 2:13 But we ought always to thank God for you, brothers loved by the Lord, because from the beginning God chose you to be saved through the sanctifying work of the Spirit and through belief in the truth.

Titus 1:1 Paul, a servant of God and an apostle of Jesus Christ for the faith of God's elect and the knowledge of the truth that leads to godliness.

DAY FIFTEEN

Romans 12:2 Don't copy the behavior and customs of this world, but let God transform you into a new person by changing the way you think. Then you will learn to know God's will for you, which is good and pleasing and perfect. (NLT)

2 Corinthians 10:5 We demolish arguments and every pretension that sets itself up against the knowledge of God, and we take captive every thought to make it obedient to Christ.

Romans 5:10-11 For since our friendship with God was restored by the death of his Son while we were still his enemies, we will certainly be saved through the life of his Son. So now we can rejoice in our wonderful new relationship with God because our Lord Jesus Christ has made us friends of God. NLT

2 Corinthians 5:17-19 Therefore, if anyone is in Christ, he is a new creation; the old has gone, the new has come! All this is from God, who reconciled us to himself through Christ and gave us the ministry of reconciliation: that God was reconciling the world to himself in

Christ, not counting men's sins against them. And he has committed to us the message of reconciliation.

DAY SIXTEEN

Philippians 1:6 Being confident of this, that he who began a good work in you will carry it on to completion until the day of Christ Jesus.

Jeremiah 29:11 For I know the plans I have for you," declares the LORD, "plans to prosper you and not to harm you, plans to give you hope and a future.

2 Peter 1:3 His divine power has given us everything we need for life and godliness through our knowledge of him who called us by his own glory and goodness.

John 14:26 (NASB) But the Helper, the Holy Spirit, whom the Father will send in My name, He will teach you all things, and bring to your remembrance all that I said to you.

John 15:26 (NASB) "When the Helper comes, whom I will send to you from the Father, that is the Spirit of truth who proceeds from the Father, He will testify about Me,

Romans 8:11- And if the Spirit of him who raised Jesus from the dead is living in you, he who raised Christ from the dead will also give life to your mortal bodies through his Spirit, who lives in you.

Ephesians 4:32 (HCSB) 32 And be kind and compassionate to one another, forgiving one another, just as God also forgave you in Christ.

DAY SEVENTEEN

John 10:27-   My sheep listen to my voice; I know them, and they follow me.
Isaiah 30:21- Whether you turn to the right or to the left, your ears will hear a voice behind you, saying, "This is the way; walk in it."

Romans 8:1- Therefore, there is now no condemnation for those who are in Christ Jesus.

Romans 8:1- With the arrival of Jesus, the Messiah, that fateful dilemma is resolved. Those who enter into Christ's being-here-for-us no longer have to live under a continuous, low-lying black cloud. A new power is in operation. The Spirit of life in Christ, like a strong wind, has magnificently cleared the air, freeing you from a fated lifetime of brutal tyranny at the hands of sin and death. (MSG)

Romans 8:1- Therefore, [there is] now no condemnation (no adjudging guilty of wrong) for those who are in Christ Jesus, who live [and] walk not after the dictates of the flesh, but after the dictates of the Spirit. (Amplified)

Romans 8:1- Therefore, [there is] now no condemnation (no adjudging guilty of wrong) for those who are in Christ Jesus, who live [and] walk not after the dictates of the flesh, but after the dictates of the Spirit. KJV

Romans 12:21- Do not be overcome by evil, but overcome evil with good.

DAY EIGHTEEN

Acts 16:16-34- Once when we were going to the place of prayer, we were met by a slave girl who had a spirit by which she predicted the future. She earned a great deal of money for her owners by fortune-telling. This girl followed Paul and the rest of us, shouting, "These men are servants of the Most High God, who are telling you the way to be saved." She kept this up for many days. Finally Paul became so troubled that he turned around and said to the spirit, "In the name of Jesus Christ I command you to come out of her!" At that moment the spirit left her.
When the owners of the slave girl realized that their hope of making money was gone, they seized Paul and Silas and dragged them into the marketplace to face the authorities. They brought them before the magistrates and said, "These men are Jews, and are throwing our city into an uproar by advocating customs unlawful for us Romans to accept or practice."
The crowd joined in the attack against Paul and Silas, and the magistrates ordered them to be stripped and beaten. After they had been severely flogged, they were thrown into prison, and the jailer was commanded to guard them carefully. Upon receiving such orders, he put them in the inner cell and fastened their feet in the stocks.
About midnight Paul and Silas were praying and singing hymns to God, and the other prisoners were listening to them. Suddenly there was such a violent earthquake that the foundations of the prison were shaken. At once all the prison doors flew open, and everybody's chains came loose. The jailer woke up, and when he saw the prison

doors open, he drew his sword and was about to kill himself because he thought the prisoners had escaped. But Paul shouted, "Don't harm yourself! We are all here!"
The jailer called for lights, rushed in and fell trembling before Paul and Silas. He then brought them out and asked, "Sirs, what must I do to be saved?"
They replied, "Believe in the Lord Jesus, and you will be saved—you and your household." Then they spoke the word of the Lord to him and to all the others in his house. At that hour of the night the jailer took them and washed their wounds; then immediately he and all his family were baptized. The jailer brought them into his house and set a meal before them; he was filled with joy because he had come to believe in God—he and his whole family.

Philippians 4:4- Rejoice in the Lord always. I will say it again: Rejoice!

Philippians 2:18- So you too should be glad and rejoice with me.

Philippians 3:1- Finally, my brothers, rejoice in the Lord! It is no trouble for me to write the same things to you again, and it is a safeguard for you.

DAY NINETEEN

Philippians 1:12-14- Now I want you to know, brothers, that what has happened to me has really served to advance the gospel. As a result, it has become clear throughout the whole palace guard and to everyone else that I am in chains for Christ. Because of my chains, most of the brothers in the Lord have been encouraged to speak the word of God more courageously and fearlessly.

Romans 8:28- And we know that in all things God works for the good of those who love him, who have been called according to his purpose.

Genesis 50:20- You intended to harm me, but God intended it for good to accomplish what is now being done, the saving of many lives.

Jeremiah 29:11 For I know the plans I have for you," declares the Lord, "plans to prosper you and not to harm you, plans to give you hope and a future.

DAY TWENTY

James 1:2- My brethren, count it all joy when ye fall into divers temptations; (KJV)
v. 2 - Consider it pure joy, my brothers, whenever you face trials of many kinds. (NIV)

James 1: 3-4- because you know that the testing of your faith develops perseverance. Perseverance must finish its work so that you may be mature and complete, not lacking anything.

Romans 8:29- For those God foreknew he also predestined to be conformed to the likeness of his Son, that he might be the firstborn among many brothers.

2 Corinthians 3:18- And we, who with unveiled faces all reflect the Lord's glory, are being transformed into his likeness with ever-increasing glory, which comes from the Lord, who is the Spirit.

Matthew 4:1-11- Then Jesus was led by the Spirit into the desert to be tempted by the devil. After fasting forty days and forty nights, he was hungry. The tempter came to him and said, "If you are the Son of God, tell these stones to become bread."
Jesus answered, "It is written: 'Man does not live on bread alone, but on every word that comes from the mouth of God.'"

Then the devil took him to the holy city and had him stand on the highest point of the temple. "If you are the Son of God," he said, "throw yourself down. For it is written:
" 'He will command his angels concerning you, and they will lift you up in their hands, so that you will not strike your foot against a stone.'"
Jesus answered him, "It is also written: 'Do not put the Lord your God to the test.'"
Again, the devil took him to a very high mountain and showed him all the kingdoms of the world and their splendor. "All this I will give you," he said, "if you will bow down and worship me."
Jesus said to him, "Away from me, Satan! For it is written: 'Worship the Lord your God, and serve him only.'"
Then the devil left him, and angels came and attended him.

DAY TWENTY-ONE

Lamentations 3:1-29- I am the man who has seen affliction by the rod of his wrath.
2
  He has driven me away and made me walk in darkness rather than light;
3
  indeed, he has turned his hand against me again and again, all day long.
4
  He has made my skin and my flesh grow old and has broken my bones.
5
  He has besieged me and surrounded me with bitterness and hardship.
6
  He has made me dwell in darkness like those long dead.
7
  He has walled me in so I cannot escape; he has weighed me down with chains.
8
  Even when I call out or cry for help, he shuts out my prayer.
9
  He has barred my way with blocks of stone; he has made my paths crooked.
10
   Like a bear lying in wait, like a lion in hiding,
11
   he dragged me from the path and mangled me and left me without help.
12
   He drew his bow
and made me the target for his arrows.

13

He pierced my heart
with arrows from his quiver.

7

14

I became the laughingstock of all my people; they mock me in song all day long.

15

He has filled me with bitter herbs and sated me with gall.

16

He has broken my teeth with gravel; he has trampled me in the dust.

17

I have been deprived of peace;
I have forgotten what prosperity is.

18

So I say, "My splendor is gone
and all that I had hoped from the LORD."

19

I remember my affliction and my wandering, the bitterness and the gall.

20

I well remember them,
and my soul is downcast within me.

21

Yet this I call to mind
and therefore I have hope:

22

Because of the LORD's great love we are not consumed, for his compassions never fail.

23

They are new every morning; great is your faithfulness.

24

I say to myself, "The LORD is my portion; therefore I will wait for him."

25

The LORD is good to those whose hope is in him, to the one who seeks him;

26

it is good to wait quietly
for the salvation of the LORD.

27

It is good for a man to bear the yoke while he is young.

28

Let him sit alone in silence,
for the LORD has laid it on him.

29

Let him bury his face in the dust— there may yet be hope.

DAY TWENTY-TWO

Lamentations 3:24 - I say to myself, "The LORD is my portion; therefore I will wait for him."

Psalm 8:1 O LORD, our Lord,
how majestic is your name in all the earth!

You have set your glory above the heavens.
From the lips of children and infants you have ordained praise because of your enemies,
to silence the foe and the avenger.
3
   When I consider your heavens, the work of your fingers,
the moon and the stars, which you have set in place,
4
   what is man that you are mindful of him, the son of man that you care for him?
5   [c]
   You made him a little lower than the heavenly beings   and crowned him with glory and
honor.
6
   You made him ruler over the works of your hands; you put everything under his feet:
7
   all flocks and herds,
and the beasts of the field,
8
   the birds of the air,
and the fish of the sea,
all that swim the paths of the seas.
9
   O LORD, our Lord,
how majestic is your name in all the earth.

DAY TWENTY-THREE

1 Samuel 30:1-6- *David and his men reached Ziklag on the third day. Now the Amalekites
had raided the Negev and Ziklag. They had attacked Ziklag and burned it, and had taken
captive the women and all who were in it, both young and old. They killed none of them, but
carried them off as they went on their way.*
 *When David and his men came to Ziklag, they found it destroyed by fire and their wives and
sons and daughters taken captive. So David and his men wept aloud until they had no
strength left to weep. David's two wives had been captured—Ahinoam of Jezreel and
Abigail, the widow of Nabal of Carmel. David was greatly distressed because the men were
talking of stoning him; each one was bitter in spirit because of his sons and daughters. (8)
But David found strength in the LORD his God.*

1 Samuel 30:17-19- David fought them from dusk until the evening of the next day, and none of them got away, except four hundred young men who rode off on camels and fled. 18 David recovered everything the Amalekites had taken, including his two wives. 19 Nothing was missing: young or old, boy or girl, plunder or anything else they had taken. David brought everything back.

Psalm 139:23- 24- Search me, O God, and know my heart; test me and know my anxious thoughts.
See if there is any offensive way in me, and lead me in the way everlasting.

DAY TWENTY-FOUR

Genesis 39:2-4 The Lord was with Joseph so that he prospered, and he lived in the house of his Egyptian master. 3 When his master saw that the Lord was with him and that the Lord gave him success in everything he did, 4 Joseph found favor in his eyes and became his attendant. Potiphar put him in charge of his household, and he entrusted to his care everything he owned.

Daniel 6:21-22 (HCSB) Then Daniel spoke with the king: "May the king live forever. 22 My God sent His angel and shut the lions' mouths. They haven't hurt me, for I was found innocent before Him. Also, I have not committed a crime against you my king."

Judges 6:16 The Lord answered, "I will be with you, and you will strike down all the Midianites, leaving none alive."

DAY TWENTY-FIVE

Psalm 63:1- O God, you are my God, earnestly I seek you;
my soul thirsts for you,
my body longs for you,
in a dry and weary land where there is no water.

Isaiah 58:11- The LORD will guide you always;
he will satisfy your needs in a sun-scorched land and will strengthen your frame.
You will be like a well-watered garden,
like a spring whose waters never fail.

2

Psalm 42:1-2- As the deer pants for streams of water, so my soul pants for you, O God. My soul thirsts for God, for the living God. When can I go and meet with God?

Isaiah 65:24 Before they call I will answer; while they are still speaking I will hear.

Psalm 73:28 But as for me, it is good to be near God.
I have made the Sovereign Lord my refuge;
I will tell of all your deeds.

John 7:37-39- On the last and greatest day of the Feast, Jesus stood and said in a loud voice, "If anyone is thirsty, let him come to me and drink. Whoever believes in me, as the Scripture has said, streams of living water will flow from within him." By this he meant the Spirit, whom those who believed in him were later to receive. Up to that time the Spirit had not been given, since Jesus had not yet been glorified.

DAY TWENTY-SIX

Acts 7:57-59- At this they covered their ears and, yelling at the top of their voices, they all
58
rushed at him,   dragged him out of the city and began to stone him. Meanwhile, the witnesses laid their clothes at the feet of a young man named Saul.
59
   While they were stoning him, Stephen prayed, "Lord Jesus, receive my spirit." Acts 8:1-3-
1
  And Saul was there, giving approval to his death.

Acts 8:1-3 On that day a great persecution broke out against the church at Jerusalem, and
2
all except the apostles were scattered throughout Judea and Samaria.   Godly men buried
3
Stephen and mourned deeply for him.   But Saul began to destroy the church. Going from house to house, he dragged off men and women and put them in prison.

Acts 9:1-2- Meanwhile, Saul was still breathing out murderous threats against the Lord's disciples. He went to the high priest and asked him for letters to the synagogues in Damascus, so that if he found any there who belonged to the Way, whether men or women, he might take them as prisoners to Jerusalem.

Acts 9:3-31- As he neared Damascus on his journey, suddenly a light from heaven flashed
4
around him.   He fell to the ground and heard a voice say to him, "Saul, Saul, why do you persecute me?"
5
  "Who are you, Lord?" Saul asked.

"I am Jesus, whom you are persecuting," he replied.   "Now get up and go into the city, and you will be told what you must do."

7

  The men traveling with Saul stood there speechless; they heard the sound but did not see

8

anyone. Saul got up from the ground, but when he opened his eyes he could see nothing.

9

So they led him by the hand into Damascus.   For three days he was blind, and did not eat or drink anything.

10

  In Damascus there was a disciple named Ananias. The Lord called to him in a vision, "Ananias!" "Yes, Lord," he answered.

11

  The Lord told him, "Go to the house of Judas on Straight Street and ask for a man from

12

Tarsus named Saul, for he is praying.   In a vision he has seen a man named Ananias come and place his hands on him to restore his sight."

13

  "Lord," Ananias answered, "I have heard many reports about this man and all the harm he

14

has done to your saints in Jerusalem.   And he has come here with authority from the chief priests to arrest all who call on your name."

15

  But the Lord said to Ananias, "Go! This man is my chosen instrument to carry my name

16

before the Gentiles and their kings and before the people of Israel.   I will show him how much he must suffer for my name."

17

  Then Ananias went to the house and entered it. Placing his hands on Saul, he said, "Brother Saul, the Lord— Jesus, who appeared to you on the road as you were coming here—has sent me so that you may see again and be filled with the Holy Spirit."

18

  Immediately, something like scales fell from Saul's eyes, and he could see again. He got

19

up and was baptized,   and after taking some food, he regained his strength.

20

Saul spent several days with the disciples in Damascus.   At once he began to preach in

21

the synagogues that Jesus is the Son of God.   All those who heard him were astonished and asked, "Isn't he the man who raised havoc in Jerusalem among those who call on this

22

name? And hasn't he come here to take them as prisoners to the chief priests?"   Yet Saul grew more and more powerful and baffled the Jews living in Damascus by proving that Jesus is the Christ.

After many days had gone by, the Jews conspired to kill him,   but Saul learned of their

plan. Day and night they kept close watch on the city gates in order to kill him.   But his
followers took him by night and lowered him in a basket through an opening in the wall.
When he came to Jerusalem, he tried to join the disciples, but they were all afraid of him,

not believing that he really was a disciple.   But Barnabas took him and brought him to the
apostles. He told them how Saul on his journey had seen the Lord and that the Lord had
spoken to him, and how in Damascus he had preached fearlessly in the name of Jesus.
So Saul stayed with them and moved about freely in Jerusalem, speaking boldly in the

name of the Lord.   He talked and debated with the Grecian Jews, but they tried to kill him.
When the brothers learned of this, they took him down to Caesarea and sent him off to
Tarsus.
Then the church throughout Judea, Galilee and Samaria enjoyed a time of peace. It was
strengthened; and encouraged by the Holy Spirit, it grew in numbers, living in the fear of the
Lord.

Colossians 4:7-18 Tychicus will tell you all the news about me. He is a dear brother, a
faithful minister and fellow servant in the Lord. 8 I am sending him to you for the express
purpose that you may know about our circumstances and that he may encourage your
hearts. 9 He is coming with Onesimus, our faithful and dear brother, who is one of you. They
will tell you everything that is happening here.

10 My fellow prisoner Aristarchus sends you his greetings, as does Mark, the cousin of
Barnabas. (You have received instructions about him; if he comes to you, welcome him.) 11
Jesus, who is called Justus, also sends greetings. These are the only Jews[c] among my co-
workers for the kingdom of God, and they have proved a comfort to me. 12 Epaphras, who
is one of you and a servant of Christ Jesus, sends greetings. He is always wrestling in
prayer for you, that you may stand firm in all the will of God, mature and fully assured. 13 I
vouch for him that he is working hard for you and for those at Laodicea and Hierapolis. 14
Our dear friend Luke, the doctor, and Demas send greetings. 15 Give my greetings to the
brothers and sisters at Laodicea, and to Nympha and the church in her house.

16 After this letter has been read to you, see that it is also read in the church of the
Laodiceans and that you in turn read the letter from Laodicea.

17 Tell Archippus: "See to it that you complete the ministry you have received in the Lord."

18 I, Paul, write this greeting in my own hand. Remember my chains. Grace be with you.

Philippians 1:3-8- I thank my God every time I remember you. ⁴ In all my prayers for all of you, I always pray with joy ⁵ because of your partnership in the gospel from the first day until now, ⁶ being confident of this, that he who began a good work in you will carry it on to completion until the day of Christ Jesus. ⁷ It is right for me to feel this way about all of you, since I have you in my heart; for whether I am in chains or defending and confirming the gospel, all of you share in God's grace with me. ⁸ God can testify how I long for all of you with the affection of Christ Jesus.

DAY TWENTY-SEVEN

Galatians 6:2- Bear one another's burdens, and thereby fulfill the law of Christ. (NASV)
2 Carry each other's burdens, and in this way you will fulfill the law of Christ. (NIV)
2 Share each other's burdens, and in this way obey the law of Christ. (NLT)
Ecclesiastes 4:9-12- Two are better than one, because they have a good return for their work:
If one falls down,his friend can help him up. But pity the man who falls and has no one to help him up!
Also, if two lie down together, they will keep warm. But how can one keep warm alone?
Though one may be overpowered, two can defend themselves.
A cord of three strands is not quickly broken.

Proverbs 27:17 As iron sharpens iron, so one man sharpens another.

DAY TWENTY-EIGHT

Isaiah 7:14- Therefore the Lord himself will give you a sign: The virgin will be with child and will give birth to a son, and will call him Immanuel.

Matthew 1:23- "The virgin will be with child and will give birth to a son, and they will call him Immanuel"—which means, "God with us."

Revelation 3:20- Here I am! I stand at the door and knock. If anyone hears my voice and opens the door, I will come in and eat with him, and he with me.
Genesis 39 Now Joseph had been taken down to Egypt. Potiphar, an Egyptian who was one of Pharaoh's officials, the captain of the guard, bought him from the Ishmaelites who had taken him there.

²

The LORD was with Joseph and he prospered, and he lived in the house of his Egyptian
master. ³ When his master saw that the LORD was with him and that the LORD gave him
success in everything he did, ⁴ Joseph found favor in his eyes and became his attendant.
Potiphar put him in charge of his household, and he entrusted to his care everything he
owned. ⁵ From the time he put him in charge of his household and of all that he owned, the
LORD blessed the household of the Egyptian because of Joseph. The blessing of the LORD
was on everything Potiphar had, both in the house and in the field. ⁶ So he left in Joseph's
care everything he had; with Joseph in charge, he did not concern himself with anything
except the food he ate.

Now Joseph was well-built and handsome, ⁷ and after a while his master's wife took notice
of Joseph and said, "Come to bed with me!"
⁸ But he refused. "With me in charge," he told her, "my master does not concern himself
with anything in the house; everything he owns he has entrusted to my care. ⁹ No one is
greater in this house than I am. My master has withheld nothing from me except you,
because you are his wife. How then could I do such a wicked thing and sin against God?" ¹⁰
And though she spoke to Joseph day after day, he refused to go to bed with her or even be
with her.
16
¹¹ One day he went into the house to attend to his duties, and none of the household
servants was inside. ¹² She caught him by his cloak and said, "Come to bed with me!" But
he left his cloak in her hand and ran out of the house.
¹³ When she saw that he had left his cloak in her hand and had run out of the house, ¹⁴
she called her household servants. "Look," she said to them, "this Hebrew has been brought
to us to make sport of us! He came in here to sleep with me, but I screamed. ¹⁵ When he
heard me scream for help, he left his cloak beside me and ran out of the house."
¹⁶ She kept his cloak beside her until his master came home. ¹⁷ Then she told him this
story: "That Hebrew slave you brought us came to me to make sport of me. ¹⁸ But as soon
as I screamed for help, he left his cloak beside me and ran out of the house."

140

19

When his master heard the story his wife told him, saying, "This is how your slave treated
20
me," he burned with anger.   Joseph's master took him and put him in prison, the place
where the king's prisoners were confined.
21
But while Joseph was there in the prison,   the LORD was with him; he showed him
22
kindness and granted him favor in the eyes of the prison warden.   So the warden put
Joseph in charge of all those held in the prison, and he was made responsible for all that
23
was done there.   The warden paid no attention to anything under Joseph's care, because
the LORD was with Joseph and gave him success in whatever he did.
Genesis 41:38- So Pharaoh asked them, "Can we find anyone like this man, one in whom
is the spirit of God?"

Psalm 23:4 NLT
Even when I walk
   through the darkest valley,
I will not be afraid,
   for you are close beside me.
Your rod and your staff
   protect and comfort me.

DAY TWENTY-NINE

1 Samuel 22:1- David left Gath and escaped to the cave of Adullam. When his brothers
and his father's household heard about it, they went down to him there.
Psalm 57- Have mercy on me, O God, have mercy on me, for in you my soul takes refuge.
I will take refuge in the shadow of your wings
until the disaster has passed.
2
   I cry out to God Most High,
to God, who fulfills {his purpose} for me.
3
   He sends from heaven and saves me, rebuking those who hotly pursue me; Selah
God sends his love and his faithfulness.
4
   I am in the midst of lions;
I lie among ravenous beasts—
men whose teeth are spears and arrows, whose tongues are sharp swords.
5
   Be exalted, O God, above the heavens; let your glory be over all the earth.

6
They spread a net for my feet— I was bowed down in distress. They dug a pit in my path—
14
but they have fallen into it themselves. Selah
7
My heart is steadfast, O God, my heart is steadfast;
I will sing and make music.
8
Awake, my soul!
Awake, harp and lyre!
I will awaken the dawn.
9
I will praise you, O Lord, among the nations; I will sing of you among the peoples.
10
For great is your love, reaching to the heavens; your faithfulness reaches to the skies.
11
Be exalted, O God, above the heavens; let your glory be over all the earth.

1 Thessalonians 5:24- The one who calls you is faithful and he will do it.

DAY THIRTY

1 Kings 3: 5-15 NIV
5 At Gibeon the Lord appeared to Solomon during the night in a dream, and God said, "Ask for whatever you want me to give you."

6 Solomon answered, "You have shown great kindness to your servant, my father David, because he was faithful to you and righteous and upright in heart. You have continued this great kindness to him and have given him a son to sit on his throne this very day.

7 "Now, Lord my God, you have made your servant king in place of my father David. But I am only a little child and do not know how to carry out my duties. 8 Your servant is here among the people you have chosen, a great people, too numerous to count or number. 9 So give your servant a discerning heart to govern your people and to distinguish between right and wrong. For who is able to govern this great people of yours?"

10 The Lord was pleased that Solomon had asked for this. 11 So God said to him, "Since you have asked for this and not for long life or wealth for yourself, nor have asked for the death of your enemies but for discernment in administering justice, 12 I will do what you have asked. I will give you a wise and discerning heart, so that there will never have been anyone like you, nor will there ever be. 13 Moreover, I will give you what you have not asked for—both wealth and honor—so that in your lifetime you will have no equal among kings. 14 And if you walk in obedience to me and keep my decrees and commands as David your

father did, I will give you a long life." 15 Then Solomon awoke—and he realized it had been a dream.

He returned to Jerusalem, stood before the ark of the Lord's covenant and sacrificed burnt offerings and fellowship offerings. Then he gave a feast for all his court.

James 1:5 If any of you lacks wisdom, you should ask God, who gives generously to all without finding fault, and it will be given to you.

Unless otherwise noted, scriptures listed are in the NIV Bible.

Author Bio:

Jeanne Hewitt teaches about how knowing Jesus is the most important thing.

Her storytelling will touch your emotions and make you want to hear more. This creative ability, woven together with years of leading Women's and Children's Ministries make Jeanne a much enjoyed Bible Study teacher and writer.☐ She is passionate about the truth of God's word.

Jeanne loves life in Kearney, MO with her husband John. They are often visited by their children, Phillip, Maggie, and Nathan. Jude, Jade, and Jack visit regularly, too, but instead of calling them grandchildren, Papa has dubbed them "*The Decibels*".☐

Made in the USA
Columbia, SC
05 June 2021